Editor-in-Chief and Founder:
    Lyndon H. LaRouche, Jr.
Editorial Board: *Lyndon H. LaRouche, Jr. , Helga
    Zepp-LaRouche, Robert Ingraham, Tony
    Papert, Gerald Rose, Dennis Small, Jeffrey
    Steinberg, William Wertz*
Co-Editors: *Robert Ingraham, Tony Papert*
Managing Editor: *Nancy Spannaus*
Technology: *Marsha Freeman*
Books: *Katherine Notley*
Ebooks: *Richard Burden*
Graphics: *Alan Yue*
Photos: *Stuart Lewis*
Circulation Manager: *Stanley Ezrol*

INTELLIGENCE DIRECTORS
Counterintelligence: *Jeffrey Steinberg, Michele
    Steinberg*
Economics: *John Hoefle, Marcia Merry Baker,
    Paul Gallagher*
History: *Anton Chaitkin*
Ibero-America: *Dennis Small*
Russia and Eastern Europe: *Rachel Douglas*
United States: *Debra Freeman*

INTERNATIONAL BUREAUS
Bogotá: *Miriam Redondo*
Berlin: *Rainer Apel*
Copenhagen: *Tom Gillesberg*
Houston: *Harley Schlanger*
Lima: *Sara Madueño*
Melbourne: *Robert Barwick*
Mexico City: *Gerardo Castilleja Chávez*
New Delhi: *Ramtanu Maitra*
Paris: *Christine Bierre*
Stockholm: *Ulf Sandmark*
United Nations, N.Y.C.: *Leni Rubinstein*
Washington, D.C.: *William Jones*
Wiesbaden: *Göran Haglund*

ON THE WEB
e-mail: eirns@larouchepub.com
www.larouchepub.com
www.executiveintelligencereview.com
www.larouchepub.com/eiw
Webmaster: *John Sigerson*
Assistant Webmaster: *George Hollis*
Editor, Arabic-language edition: *Hussein Askary*

EIR (ISSN 0273-6314) *is published weekly
(50 issues), by EIR News Service, Inc.,
P.O. Box 17390, Washington, D.C. 20041-0390.
(703) 297-8434*

European Headquarters: E.I.R. GmbH, Postfach
Bahnstrasse 9a, D-65205, Wiesbaden, Germany
Tel: 49-611-73650
Homepage: http://www.eir.de
e-mail: info@eir.de
Director: Georg Neudecker

Montreal, Canada: 514-461-1557
eir@eircanada.ca

Denmark: EIR - Danmark, Sankt Knuds Vej 11,
basement left, DK-1903 Frederiksberg, Denmark.
Tel.: +45 35 43 60 40, Fax: +45 35 43 87 57. e-mail:
eirdk@hotmail.com.

Mexico City: EIR, Sor Juana Inés de la Cruz 242-2
Col. Agricultura C.P. 11360
Delegación M. Hidalgo, México D.F.
Tel. (5525) 5318-2301
eirmexico@gmail.com

Copyright: ©2017 EIR News Service. All rights
reserved. Reproduction in whole or in part without
permission strictly prohibited.

Canada Post Publication Sales Agreement
#40683579

Postmaster: Send all address changes to *EIR*, P.O.
Box 17390, Washington, D.C. 20041-0390.

Signed articles in *EIR* represent the views of the authors,
and not necessarily those of the Editorial Board.

The Grand Design for The Next 50 Years

The Optimism of the American Presidency

by Robert Ingraham

Nov. 4—As this article goes to press, President Trump has just embarked on his twelve-day tour of Asia, a trip which will include participation in both the APEC Economic Leaders' Meeting and the ASEAN summit; visits to Japan, China, Korea, the Philippines, and Vietnam; and personal meetings with President Xi Jinping of China and other heads of state, probably including Russia's President Vladimir Putin.

The most important component of the President's trip will be his Nov. 8-10 visit to China and the discussions between the Chinese and American Presidents. These discussions will commence less than three weeks after the conclusion of the 19th Congress of the Communist Party of China (CPC), a Congress which incorporated the economic philosophy of the Belt and Road (or New Silk Road) Initiative (BRI) into the Constitution of the CPC. Under President Xi's direction, China has now *constitutionally* dedicated itself to making the global development initiatives of the Belt and Road the foundation for all Chinese economic policy.

We are at an historic moment of great possibilities. Opportunities abound for the complete eradication of cold-war geopolitics in U.S.A.-Chinese relations, and the door is wide open for American participation in the projects of the Belt and Road. The combination of the decisions taken at the 19th Party Congress, together with new potential arising from the President's Asia trip, anticipates a new era of global cooperation and the greatest world-wide physical economic development in the history of the human species. The opportunity for a breakthrough in relations between the two nations was clearly signaled by an editorial, "China, U.S. presidents to map out future relations," which appeared in the official press agency of the People's Republic of China, Xinhua, this morning.

The era of trans-Atlantic triumphalism following the dissolution of the Soviet Union in 1991 is now crumbling. Even in the earliest days of his presidential campaign—in 2015 and 2016—Donald Trump was explicit that his intention was to end the sixteen years of Permanent War which our nation suffered through under the Bush and Obama Presidencies—to end the policy of regime change, to reject military adventurism, and to rebuild relations with both Russia and China. Since his inauguration, Trump's friendly initiatives to both Vladimir Putin and Xi Jinping have given proof that this stated intention was not mere campaign rhetoric. It is precisely the President's determination to pursue such a dramatic strategic shift that has put him in the cross-hairs of the London-Wall Street trans-Atlantic oligarchy,—their rabid desire to remove him from office—and it is certainly no coincidence that the first indictments handed down by Special Counsel Robert Mueller occurred only four days before President Trump departed for Asia.

Understanding the American Presidency

Although it is often overlooked or misunderstood by many, a key ingredient which could lead to the success of President Trump's current initiatives lies in the nature of the American Presidency itself. It might strike some as incongruous to interrupt a discussion of current strategic matters with historical observations on the Presidency; yet a properly understood strategic understanding of the constitutional American Presidency is crucial to appreciating the potential for victory in the current environment.

Unlike the leaders of many nations, the U.S. President is neither a partisan figure—representing only the program of one particular party—nor is he beholden to the dictates of any parliamentary or legislative majority. Constitutionally, the President has only one charge: to represent in his or her person the principles enunciated in the Preamble of the United States Constitution, and, by so doing, to lead the nation toward a better future. No faction, no special interest, no Congressional obstruction, and certainly not the news media, are allowed to prevent the President from carrying out that Constitutional obligation.

At the time of the Constitutional Convention in 1787, the majority of the delegates supported James Madison's Virginia Plan that would have created a figure-head presidency, one elected by Congress and stripped of all but ceremonial power. Alexander Hamilton's intervention on June 18 that year prevented this. Hamilton's plan authorized the President to make all foreign treaties, to make all important executive appointments, to have broad powers to pardon anyone of a crime, to be Commander in Chief of the Armed Forces, and to veto legislation. It also removed the state governments and the Congress from any role in selecting the President, establishing instead an independent Electoral College,—elected directly by the people—from which Congressmen and other public officials were strictly excluded.

In the closing days of the Convention, it would be Gouverneur Morris who would accomplish the inclusion of many of Hamilton's proposals. On Aug. 31, Morris succeeded in overturning the proposal for Congressional selection of the President, in favor of establishing the Electoral College system. That same week, he successfully battled for the President, not the Senate, to negotiate treaties and appoint ambassadors and Supreme Court judges. He also overturned the restriction that the President would be limited to only one term.

Hamilton and Morris were not done. In the Committee on Style, which was charged with putting the final Constitution into its finished form, they changed the wording of both Article I and Article II, drastically altering the relationship between Congress and the President. In the new wording, Congress was limited to "all legislative powers herein granted," i.e., only to those powers specifically enumerated. At the same time, nonspecific and open-ended "Executive Power shall be vested in a President of the United States."

America is a Presidential System, and the changes in the Constitution accomplished by Hamilton and Morris were not merely of form and not intended simply to make the government more efficient. On July 2, Gouverneur Morris said, "The rich will strive to establish their dominion and enslave the rest. They always did… they always will. They will have the same effect here as elsewhere, if we do not, by the power of government, keep them in their proper spheres." The Presidency, as designed by Hamilton and Morris, was the means by which to accomplish this. They were also of the view that the greatest danger to the principles of the American Revolution would arise from within Congress; that Congress, by its very nature, would become susceptible to influence from factions and would become corrupted by the might of the rich and powerful. They acted to establish the institution of the Presidency to prevent those interests from taking control of the nation, creating instead an office answerable only to the people, their posterity, and the charge of the Constitution's Preamble.

A President Speaks

For the purpose of elucidating how the American Presidency leads the nation, how it defines the purpose and future direction for nation, we provide here excerpts from George Washington's 1796 Farewell Address:

> Observe good faith and justice towards all nations; cultivate peace and harmony with all. Religion and morality enjoin this conduct; and can it be, that good policy does not equally enjoin it—It will be worthy of a free, enlightened, and at no distant period, a great nation, to give to mankind the magnanimous and too novel example of a people always guided by an exalted justice and benevolence…
>
> In the execution of such a plan, nothing is more essential than that permanent, inveterate antipathies against particular nations, and passionate attachments for others, should be excluded; and that, in place of them, just and amicable feelings towards all should be cultivated. The nation which indulges towards another a habitual hatred or a habitual fondness is in some degree a slave. It is a slave to its animosity or to its affection, either of which is sufficient to lead it astray from its duty and its interest. Antipathy in one nation against another disposes each more

readily to offer insult and injury, to lay hold of slight causes of umbrage, and to be haughty and intractable, when accidental or trifling occasions of dispute occur. Hence, frequent collisions, obstinate, envenomed, and bloody contests...

Harmony, liberal intercourse with all nations, are recommended by policy, humanity, and interest. But even our commercial policy should hold an equal and impartial hand; neither seeking nor granting exclusive favors or preferences; consulting the natural course of things; diffusing and diversifying by gentle means the streams of commerce, but forcing nothing....

Moral Challenge of the Presidency

It is the burden of the Presidency to lead the nation to a better future, a future of "life, liberty, and the pursuit of happiness." This is what we see in Washington's final message to Americans; this is the mission he accepted and from which he never wavered. There is the quality of Joan of Arc in the concept of the American Presidency, and we see in the greatest of Presidents how they accepted that mission, how they "grew" into the Office, and how new qualities of moral leadership rose up: witness Lincoln's struggle with slavery and with the heavy burden of war—and his ultimate glorious Emancipation; Franklin Roosevelt's years-long struggle with polio, leading to his crusade on behalf of the Forgotten Man and the Four Freedoms; John F. Kennedy's courageous American University address, proclaiming his intention to overturn the cold war geopolitics of Winston Churchill and Harry Truman; and Ronald Reagan's endorsement of Lyndon LaRouche's Strategic Defense Initiative, intended to end decades of the satanic policy of Mutual and Assured Destruction (MAD).

The American Presidency is not a political office. It is a mission—one to defend and further the principles and intention of the American Republic, as that Republic was established between 1776 and 1797. The quality of personal courage required to accept and shoulder that mission is perhaps best seen in Martin Luther King, Jr. On Jan. 28, 1957, King delivered a sermon wherein he described his experiences during the recent Montgomery Bus Boycott. King said:

> I went to bed many nights scared to death by threats against my family. Early on a sleepless morning in January 1956, rationality left me. Almost out of nowhere I heard a voice that morning saying to me:
>
> "Preach the Gospel, stand up for the truth, stand up for righteousness."
>
> Since that morning I can stand up without fear. So I'm not afraid of anybody this morning. Tell Montgomery they can keep shooting and I'm going to stand up to them; tell Montgomery they can keep bombing and I'm going to stand up to them.

All of the attacks on President Trump at this time are intended break him,—as the threats were intended to cow King—to drive Trump from office, to destroy the potential of the steps he is taking toward ending America's subservience to British geopolitics. Many in Congress, from both parties,—and their friends in the news media—exhibit today precisely the profound corruption of which Gouverneur Morris warned, and against which an independent Presidency was designed to defend the nation.

The President has broad, awesome, constitutional powers to defeat those who are arrayed against him. He is not beholden to Congress or any other government agency for the initiatives he is now making. This is how the Presidency was designed.

Perhaps, as you are reading this, President Trump is deep in conversation with Xi Jinping in Beijing. The enemies of humanity howl and wail, but the standard of hope has been firmly planted. Trans-Atlantic British geopolitics must die, and a better future will emerge.

EIR **Contents**

www.larouchepub.com Volume 44, Number 45, November 10, 2017

NASA

THE GRAND DESIGN FOR THE NEXT 50 YEARS

Worldwide Refugees Now Number 66 Million: 'The Next 50 Years of Our Planet'

by Helga Zepp-LaRouche

Dear German Federal President Steinmeier,

I read with great interest in your speech at the Singapore Management University on Nov. 2, that you brought up the fact that a series of lectures at six Singaporean universities is being held under the motto "Imagining the Next 50 Years—Where will we stand in 50 years?" And you commented on this with these words: "I think that's a bold approach—and it's something that we in Germany should do more often. We should look through a telescope into the future, rather than just looking at the very next day, the next annual balance sheet or the next election."

To hear that from you is certainly a breath of fresh air, and one can only hope that it is strong enough to blow over to the coalition negotiations in Berlin!

On the occasion of your Singapore speech, I would like to send you the book written by my husband, Lyndon LaRouche, entitled *Earth's Next 50 Years*, which he authored in 2004. In this book, he anticipates the whole currently visible shift of strategic momentum toward Eurasia, and defines the higher level of thinking with which peaceful cooperation among humanity can come to pass. Incidentally, this book is very popular in many Asian countries.

The same day that you delivered your speech to students in Singapore, UN refugee agency High Commissioner Filippo Grandi spoke in front of the UN Security Council in New York, pointing to the alarming worldwide increase in refugee numbers from 42 million in 2009 to 66 million people today, an increase of almost 70%. That's almost as many people as live in Germany! Grandi made an urgent appeal to the Security Council to do more to address the root causes of the refugee crisis: competing interests are being settled through proxy warfare rather than diplomacy and dialogue, he said, and the focus is on short-term interests rather than long-term collective stability. "Have we become unable to broker peace?" he challenged the Security Council members. This concerns the fate of millions of traumatized children who have witnessed terrible atrocities, who have been deprived of education, and who face an uncertain future; it's about women who can hardly care for their children, and elderly people who will have to die in a country not their own.

So the crucial question for humanity is: can the world community reverse this trend, find a humanist solution to the refugee issue, and establish real peace? In this regard, you too are personally challenged, as a former Foreign Minister and current Federal President of an important country.

Then, in your speech in Singapore, you said quite self-reflexively, "These days, many people look at the European Union or the United States and say: 'Well, this doesn't look very harmonious.' And many people look at China and see stability and economic growth—without a movement towards greater political freedom. So China poses a challenge to the West—not only an economic and geopolitical challenge, but also an ideological challenge."

This is undoubtedly true, but perhaps in a different way than many think in the West. What few in the West have begun to undertake, even in a rudimentary way, is an honest analysis of why things in the EU are not so harmonious, and to attempt to understand why there is growth and stability in China, and why the Chinese may be more politically free than most people in the West. (Okay, I can almost hear the readers groan already. I'm sorry, but we do have to go through this.)

Two days before your speech, President Xi Jinping presented his perspective for President Trump's upcoming state visit to China to the advisory board of the prestigious Tsinghua University School of Economics and Management, which also includes high-ranking U.S. citizens. The development of China, he stated, which has both reaped the benefits of globalization and contributed to its success, is a great opportunity for the world. The opening of China does not represent a zero-sum game, but rather the chance for win-win cooperation. During President Trump's upcoming state visit, he went on, China is ready to work with the U.S. and look far into the future, setting high goals, taking mutual interests and concerns into account, and working together to facilitate mutually beneficial cooperation between the two countries. China will seek a community for the shared future of humanity.

China has been developing ideas for the future of the next 50 years, at least since President Xi Jinping's inauguration in 2012. That was the main theme at the 19th Congress of the Communist Party, which has just taken place. There, Xi developed the perspective for shaping a better and more beautiful future, not just for China, but for the whole world.

However, Xi has always emphasized that China does not intend to export its political and social model to other countries (as the West is constantly trying to do), but only to help in their economic development through investment in infrastructure, industry and agriculture. With the Silk Road Initiative over the past four years, Xi has launched the largest infrastructure program in history, in which 70 states are already cooperating. It is undoubtedly the most important strategic initiative, because in its conception of mutually benefically cooperation lies the basis for overcoming geopolitics.

In view of the negative coverage of Trump in the German media (Second TV Channel ARD: 98% negative comments), it is perhaps surprising for the people here in Germany that both President Trump (who speaks of the relationship between President Xi and himself as the best between any two presidents) and his White House chief of staff, John Kelly, have a much more tolerant relationship with China. Kelly underscored in an interview with Fox TV that it was not the job of the U.S. to judge Beijing. China obviously has a system of government that works for the Chinese people, he added.

The Chinese newspaper *Global Times*, which is close to the government, commented on this interview by saying that what Kelly said was not something the Western elites wanted to hear from a senior member of the U.S. administration. *Global Times* continued:

For a long time, some Americans and Western people have been brainwashed by the Cold War era. They have lost the ability to assess and em-

brace the new reality. In a fast-paced world, China-U.S. relations have evolved differently from the previous mind-set. But they cannot understand the new world order at all and still measure relations between the two nations with an old yardstick. The old way of thinking is stubborn. . . .

Speaking to the Tunisian Parliament, the President of the European Parliament, Antonio Tajani has just pledged that the EU plans to increase the budget for investment in Africa from the current €3.7 bili 3.7 billion euros to 40 billion. In his view, Europe must opt for a true Marshall Plan for Africa if it wants to prevent millions of people from coming to Tunisia and continuing further. Mere words cannot convince migrants to stay at home, he said, they must have the chance for a decent life.

"Ye come late, but ye come," one can only say along with Illo from *Wallenstein*; if the EU finally adopts a more reasonable Africa policy, one could only welcome it. But if this is only based on the old mind-set, that one must counter the Silk Road policy of the Chinese in Africa with "our own path," as some Europeans have said, then this attempt will fail. Because the "spirit of the New Silk Road" is contagious, whereas insisting on bureaucratic rules that hide geopolitical intentions is not.

Now that some of the machinations of the Democratic Party leadership and Hillary Clinton's election campaign have come to light in the U.S.—manipulation from above instead of democracy, and collusion with British and U.S. intelligence services against the political opponent, Trump—it is high time that we not only rethink what is not harmonious in the Western system, but also why the Chinese system has led to growth and stability. The ideological challenge with respect to China that you speak of, involves recognizing that emphasis on the common good may represent a value just as high as individual freedom. And this does not have to be a contradiction if, like Friedrich Schiller, one thinks that freedom lies in necessity.

If, as a Federal President, you want to give a signal for the next 50 years, then you should take up and welcome China's offer for cooperation in the New Silk Road!

Best regards,
Helga Zepp-LaRouche

Helga Zepp-LaRouche is the founder of the Schiller Institutes.

The New Silk Road: Succeed with Win-Win Cooperation with China

This is a transcript of the opening address by the founder of the Schiller Institutes and chairwoman of the German Schiller Institute, Helga Zepp-LaRouche, to the Paris seminar cosponsored by the Schiller Institute in France and the Académie de Géopolitique de Paris, on Tuesday, Oct. 24.

An edited transcript of her remarks follow. See the video of her address, along with the video of Solidarité et Progrès President Jacques Cheminade's presentation.

Helga Zepp-LaRouche

Helga Zepp-LaRouche: Ladies and Gentlemen, Excellencies, Dear Guests: I would like to approach the China question from the standpoint that there is, right now, a total clash between what I would call the old paradigm and the new paradigm, and that new paradigm has been very little understood in the West. I would like to start by talking about the event that just happened in China, the 19th National Congress of the Communist Party of China (CPC) and especially the perspective outlined by President Xi Jinping for the next 35 years.

First, you should know that I was in China for the first time in 1971 in the middle of the Cultural Revolution, and therefore I have the advantage of having seen first-hand the absolutely incredible development of the Chinese miracle. China has developed in the last 40 years, since Deng Xiaoping's reforms, through the most incredible economic transformation of any country on the planet. It has lifted 700 million people out of poverty over the last 30 years. It now has a growing middle class of people who are doing very well economically, and it has the perspective of eliminating all poverty by 2020, which is only three years from now, for the remaining 42 million poor people in rural areas.

What Xi Jinping did first in his speech, was to review what has happened in the last five years, since he became General Secretary of the CPC: He developed the inner and western regions of China, and that was very difficult, because these areas are mostly desert. It was a tremendous challenge. But China has done an incredible job in doing exactly that.

One year after Xi Jinping had become General Secretary, he announced in 2013 the New Silk Road, the Belt and Road Initiative (BRI), in Kazakhstan, and in the four years since this project was put on the agenda, again, the most breathtaking development has taken place, where now, about 70 countries are actively participating in this project.

Xi announced that by 2020, China should be a moderately prosperous country; by 2035 China should be fully modernized, and by 2050 it's supposed to have become a "strong, democratic, culturally advanced, harmonious and beautiful nation." Xi emphasized that in China's development, they were adding miracle upon miracle, and were drawing on the 5,000 years of China's history, in which China contributed many advances to humankind, and were also developing a spirit of science, of innovation, and excellence for the future. He mentioned fourteen times in his speech that the aim of all of this is that people would have a better and a happy life. Now, I have not heard that said from any Western politician for a very long time. It is in the U.S. Declaration of Independence that the "pursuit of happiness" is an inalienable right of all people, but if I look at the political processes in Europe or the United States, "happiness" is not a subject of discussion as the purpose of policies.

What China has done is to take the Chinese economic miracle, and offer it through the Belt and Road Initiative to all participating countries, and that has al-

ready transformed all of Asia, much of Europe, Eastern Europe, Southern Europe, Africa, and Latin America. At this Party Congress, there were many foreign leaders who said they will now take the inspiration of the Chinese model for their own development.

While this has been happening in China, you have had a peak of unprecedented attacks on China in the Western media. In Bloomberg, *Time* magazine, and the *Wall Street Journal*, you had a barrage of articles accusing China of merely attempting to gain global power, to replace Anglo-American imperialism with Chinese imperialism; that it's a grab for raw materials; that Xi Jinping is like Stalin, like Mao Zedong. They stop at nothing with their accusations.

So, why is it that the countries that are participating with China in the Belt and Road, 70 countries or maybe even more than 100, are all happy, that they all praise what China is doing? How can it be that there is such a complete difference in perception of what is going on? This is what I call the clash between the old paradigm and the new paradigm, because what China is offering is "win-win cooperation." Of course China is pursuing its own interests, but it is also acting in the interest of the participating countries; so there's a mutual benefit for both sides.

We've Fought for It for 26 Years

Let's take it back a little bit: When the Soviet Union approached its last phase, in the United States the neocons developed a concept which they called the Project for a New American Century (PNAC), which was the idea that there should only be a unipolar world, domi-

nated by the Anglo-Americans.

When the Wall in Berlin came down, my husband Lyndon LaRouche's movement had an answer: We proposed the "Productive Triangle," economic development linking Paris, Berlin and Vienna. This was the idea of transforming the Comecon countries with Western technologies through development corridors. In 1991, when the Soviet Union disintegrated, the Iron Curtain was down, and we proposed the "Eurasian Land-Bridge," which was the idea of connecting the population and industrial centers of Europe with those of Asia through development corridors, and in 1991, we called that the "New Silk Road."

We have campaigned for this over 26 years, but of course, if you go back to '91, this idea was not in the interests of the Bush Sr. Administration; or of Margaret Thatcher, who called German unification the "Fourth Reich"; or even of French President Mitterrand, who opposed German reunification, so there were many geopolitical obstacles to realizing this plan at that time.

The unipolar world forces then began to pursue their policy, which consists of regime change against any country, any government, that opposes the unipolar world, of color revolution, and of such concepts as the "right to protect" (R2P) to conduct interventionist wars under the pretext of fighting for human rights and democracy. That policy has given us the mess in the Middle East and the refugee crisis. This was what ensued over these past decades.

That military-strategic policy was combined with an economic policy which caused the lack of development as a result of the IMF conditionalities, which explicitly prevented Third World development. The policy of the Troika in Europe similarly prescribed brutal austerity to Southern European countries such as Greece, Italy, Spain, and Portugal. This led to the revolts against this system which we have been watching for the past two years. That revolt expressed itself in the Brexit, in the election victory of President Trump and the loss of Hillary Clinton, in the "no" to the referendum in Italy for the change in the Constitution; and in recent developments such as the election victory of Kurz in Austria and Babic in the Czech Republic, as well as the eruption in Catalonia—so this is an ongoing revolt.

That policy is now leading to the danger of a new financial crisis, much worse than 2008, because the causes of that crisis have not been addressed. To the contrary, through quantitative easing and negative interest rates, an enormous amount of liquidity was pumped into the system which manifests itself now in the form of a much, much bigger indebtedness of governments, of firms, of student debt, and of car loans— and this is a bubble about to explode again.

China is not unaware of the reaction of the Western media towards the Chinese model. I find it very interesting that in recent days there has been a completely new tone in the Chinese media about this reaction from the West. They say, with a very new self-confidence—less diplomatically than the Chinese usually speak—that their model is superior to the Western model. And they talk about the errors of Western conceptions about China, that the West completely misses the true nature of Chinese development, that the West obviously does not want China to succeed, and predicts that it will not succeed. One article says that the West thinks that the closer that China is to the West, the more they're on the right path; if it diverges, it's dangerous; that China should support the interests of the West, and therefore that China's development is negative and challenges the world order; and that China should not challenge what they call "universal values." But in reality these "universal values" are just Western interests. And then, in several articles, they say, look at the chaos in the West: the influence of the Western media is shrinking and China should no longer care about Western prejudices.

So, I'm just touching upon these things, because it is my firm belief that the New Silk Road dynamic is unstoppable, because it is the much more attractive model of international cooperation, and it will eventually be put on the table in all of Europe. I think it would be in the fundamental interests of European nations to cooperate with China and with Russia in the development of Africa: This is the only human way to stop and overcome the refugee crisis. China has offered "win-win cooperation" to [German Chancellor] Mrs. Merkel, to [Italy's Prime Minister] Gentiloni, and to [former French Prime Minister] Mr. Raffarin, when he was at

Chinese President Xi Jinping, foreign delegation heads, and guests, after the first session of the Leaders' Roundtable Summit at the Belt and Road Forum for International Cooperation, in Beijing, China, May 15, 2017.

the Belt and Road Forum in Beijing in May—so the offer is on the table. The same goes for the reconstruction of the war-torn countries of the Middle East, where, in the case of Syria, there is already an emerging tripartite cooperation, in which China provides the infrastructure, Russia the energy, Iran the industrial parks, and other countries are invited to cooperate in rebuilding Syria as well; and the same goes for Iraq, Afghanistan, Yemen, and other countries of the region.

Contrary to what you read in most Western mainstream media, the possibility that there will be a good relationship between Trump and Xi Jinping in the upcoming visit of President Trump to Asia—where he will go to Vietnam, Philippines, South Korea, Japan, and a state visit to China—is very good.

The whole Russia-gate against President Trump, the idea that there was collusion between the Trump team and Russia, whereby Putin allegedly helped Trump to win the election—is utter nonsense. There's no evidence for it, and it was designed entirely by the intelligence services of Great Britain and the Bush-Obama administrations, to prevent Trump from having a positive relationship with Russia and China—and that is not succeeding.

The United States is right now undergoing a tremendous economic crisis, a total collapse of infrastructure due to non-investment for about 100 years; infrastructure in the United States is collapsing. The United States has 150 km of fast rail system between New York and Boston, as compared to more than 20,000 km of fast rail systems in China, and there is right now a very concrete discussion of China, together with the Japan, investing in the infrastructure of the United States. This could be a subject in the upcoming Trump visit to China.

There are already many strategic realignments going on: I only want to point to what may be the most obvious case, that of Japan. Japan right now is seeking a very good relationship with Russia, and they are developing the Kuril Islands together economically. And because of the strategically close relationship between Xi Jinping and Putin, relations between Japan and China are improving.

I want to say in conclusion, that from the standpoint of universal history, I think that mankind has reached the point where we must move to a new paradigm of self-governance of relations among nations, and stop thinking that war can be a means of conflict resolution in the age of thermonuclear weapons—if you don't want to risk eliminating ourselves as a species.

So we have to think about a new paradigm of cooperation, and it is on the table. I think that the kind of discussion we need to have in Europe, really needs to take on a completely different shape and form. I don't even think "multipolarity" is what we want, because multipolarity still contains the idea of geopolitical confrontation, where you have one group of countries which has an interest against another group of countries. I think that the idea pronounced by President Xi Jinping of the "community of a shared future of humanity," where you start with the one mankind first, and then you come to the national or regional interest—is the way we have to think.

As a last comment, I think that the West can only find this kind of cooperation if we develop or rediscover our best traditions. As China has revived its Confucian tradition of 2,500 years, so the West has to revive the best Classical traditions of all our European cultures. If we do that, I think we are at the verge of a new era. [applause]

There was time for one question, which was raised about China's "human rights record." Here is Mrs. Zepp-LaRouche's response:

Helga Zepp-LaRouche: Would you agree with me that to die of hunger is a violation of human rights? The Swiss author Jean Ziegler has written a very good book

The Three Gorges Dam on the Yangtze River, China.

about why dying of hunger is the worst possible death, because the body eats up its own organs first, and it's associated with incredible suffering.

I think that China has the best record for human rights because they have eliminated the most poverty. They have ended poverty for 700 million people in their own country, and I think that is what provides the precondition for people to live.

It's a question of what is more important. Look at the hurricanes which have now devastated the Caribbean, Texas, Florida, the states on the Gulf of Mexico, and Puerto Rico. Are these natural catastrophes? No. Because the effect could have been lessened tremendously by having flood control, by having,— for example, Houston has no underground water system, while Tokyo has seven big reservoirs enabling flooding to be controlled. Now, China, for its part, developed the Three Gorges Dam. People freaked out at the time about the several thousand people who had to be relocated, but the *lives* of *many* thousands of people were saved, because the common good was put above narrow, individual interest.

So I think the Western idea of what people call "individual rights" is not necessarily the right conception. I think that there is a real misunderstanding. I also agree with Foreign Minister Lavrov of Russia, who recently said that the values of the West are no longer the values which were transmitted from generation to generation, but that those values have been replaced by "everything is allowed, everything goes, all sexual varieties are allowed," and Lavrov called these "post-Christian values."

I think we have a crisis of values in the West. And I think that before we judge these nations, we should really rethink who is doing something for the common good, and who not? [applause]

The New Silk Road: How China's Win-Win Approach Is Transforming the World

Seminar in Paris co-sponsored by the Schiller Institute and the Geopolitical Academy of Paris

by Christine Bierre

More than a hundred diplomats, experts, business leaders, China specialists, French-China friendship associations, parliamentary attaches, media, students of Far-East civilizations, and French citizens participated in a highly successful seminar held in Paris, on Oct. 24. It was co-organized by the Schiller Institute and the Geopolitical Academy of Paris, on the theme of how China's New Silk Road win-win approach works and how it is already transforming the world. This intense seminar covered the essentials of the Chinese project, the Confucian philosophy which inspires it, the Hamilton/List/Carey/LaRouche foundation of its economic policies, as well as concrete examples which are already working in Africa, and the recipe for joint Franco-Chinese projects in France and Europe, or abroad.

Schiller Institute

Helga Zepp-LaRouche addressing the Oct. 24 seminar in Paris.

I. Introductory Remarks by Rastbeen and Zepp-LaRouche

The seminar started with introductory remarks by Ali Rastbeen, president and founder of the Paris Academy of Geopolitics (ACP) and by Helga Zepp-LaRouche, founder of the Schiller Institutes, also known in China and in broad circles internationally, as the Silk Road Lady. "The New Silk Road will make China the leader in world trade and facilitate its trade with Western Europe, its most important partner," said Rastbeen noting that while on the one hand the project will secure China's trade routes and energy supplies, it is also an alternative to the present unipolar order. The Chinese project can transform the Middle East. "Relations between China and the Middle East are friendly; they have common visions on a number of regional and international questions, among which is peace and development." Washington's policies in the Middle East, on the contrary, limit themselves to two axes: securing its own oil resources and transport routes, and ensuring the military supremacy of its main ally in the region, Israel. Rastbeen noted however, that traditionally China has been a good commercial partner of Israel, including in the purchase of military hardware. China's Silk Road is therefore a potential venue to easing tensions and creating stability in the region.

Helga Zepp-LaRouche concentrated her remarks (see video or the previous article in this issue for a full transcript) on the far-reaching conclusions of the 19th Communist Party Congress for the future of China and the world, after first establishing her credibility on what the Chinese have accomplished so far. "I had the benefit of being in China for the first time in 1971, during the Cultural Revolution, and therefore I saw personally the most incredible changes the Chinese miracle has represented."

Since the reforms of Deng Xiao Ping, more than 40 years ago, China has realized the greatest transformation of any country on this planet. China has pulled 700 million people out of extreme poverty, and a middle class has emerged which lives very well. The goals announced by Xi Jinping at the CPC Congress, are that by 2020 China will end extreme poverty, by 2035 it will be a totally modernized country, and by 2050 it will be a "strong, democratic, culturally advanced, beautiful and harmonious nation." Mrs. LaRouche noted that throughout his speech Xi Jinping had mentioned 14 times that his objective is to provide people a better and happier life. One cannot say, she said, that the right to happiness is a political debate in our Western countries.

What China has done with its New Silk Road policy, is to take its own economic miracle and offer a win-win possibility to all participating countries to realize their own such miracle. And that policy has already transformed numerous countries in Asia, Africa, Latin America, southern and eastern Europe.

While all this is happening, however, the Western media has organized the most incredible barrage to discredit the New Silk Road, accusing China of imperialism, of wanting to hoard the world's raw materials, and

Xinhua

President Xi Jinping, walking to the podium to address the 19th Party Congress.

comparing Xi Jinping to Stalin and Mao. This is nothing but the continuation of the policy orientation adopted by the Anglo-American neo-conservatives following the collapse of the Soviet Union, she said, their will to impose a unipolar world through regime change, color revolutions, and theories like the "right to protect." The neo-liberal policies promoted in the economic domain have led to global impoverishment of the middle class and the population at large, and have provoked the Brexit, Trump, Kurz and Catalonian revolts.

For Mrs. LaRouche, there is an ongoing clash between this unipolar paradigm of civilization and the new win-win paradigm that China and Russia are trying to implement. Mrs. LaRouche outlined how she and her husband, Lyndon LaRouche, in 1991, following the final collapse of the Soviet Union, proposed to connect the European centers of population and of industrial production through industrial corridors of development, which they had called, in 1991, the Eurasian Landbridge or the New Silk Road.

I think that it is in the interest of European nations to cooperate with China and Russia in the Development of Africa, she said, calling this approach "the only humane way of dealing with the refugee crisis. We need a new paradigm of cooperation, and this one is already on the table."

II. Alternatives to War and Geopolitics

The Confucian Foundation of the New Silk Road policy

Christine Bierre

Christine Bierre

Christine Bierre, editor in chief of Nouvelle Solidarité, showed the antinomy between Geopolitics and the Chinese model of win-win relations. Unfortunately, the term Geopolitics coined in the early XXth century by two Anglo-Saxon imperialists, Halford Mackinder and Karl Haushofer which inspired Hitler's *Lebensraum*, has entirely replaced that of "strategy" today, when in reality it is merely a synonym for Might is Right.

The real inspiration for the Chinese win-win model is Confucianism, the ancient moral philosophy of the Chinese whose main value is "love for humanity" and the obligation to perfect oneself, a philosophy specially designed for the education of a virtuous public administration. But in order to understand this, she said, one must understand the Chinese society from the inside. Leibniz was the first to discover that the Western and Chinese civilizations could dialogue via Confucianism. We must today also develop this avenue of thought in order to see how close we are to the Chinese, who are presented to us today as menacing!

The French, in particular, who from ancient rulers to Charles de Gaulle often governed through the Missi Dominici, the officers of the King or the public administration of the day, should be inspired to see the role played by the "erudite" administration of civil servants in ensuring the best possible governments, in dynasties associated with Golden Age and with the strong development of the Silk Road, such as in the Han dynasty (206 BC -220 AD), the Tang dynasty (618- 957AD), and the Song dynasty (957-1259AD). Bierre went through the strong scientific, industrial and artistic development of these epochs, comparable however in many ways to the Grand Designs of Charlemagne, Colbert and Charles de Gaulle in Europe. It is by readopting our true identity that we will stop fearing China and enter a partnership with it instead.

Space: The Common Aims of Mankind in the 21st Century

Sebastien Drochon

Sebastien Drochon

The fight against geopolitics and for the common aims of mankind goes through an ambitious space exploration policy, said Sebastien Drochon of the Schiller Institute science team in France. This is a fight that we have waged for a long time, and that China is carrying out on its own.

Drochon started with a beautiful quote from the great Krafft Ehricke, the German engineer and pioneer, with Wernher von Braun, of manned space travel. Ehricke, in his "Anthropology of Astronautics" stated, "The concept of space travel carries with it enormous impact, because it challenges man on practically all fronts of his physical and spiritual existence." He believed that when confronted to the limits of a given system and forced to change, the universe gives us the means to overcome the limits.

Drochon gave an overview of the Chinese space

Yutu rover.

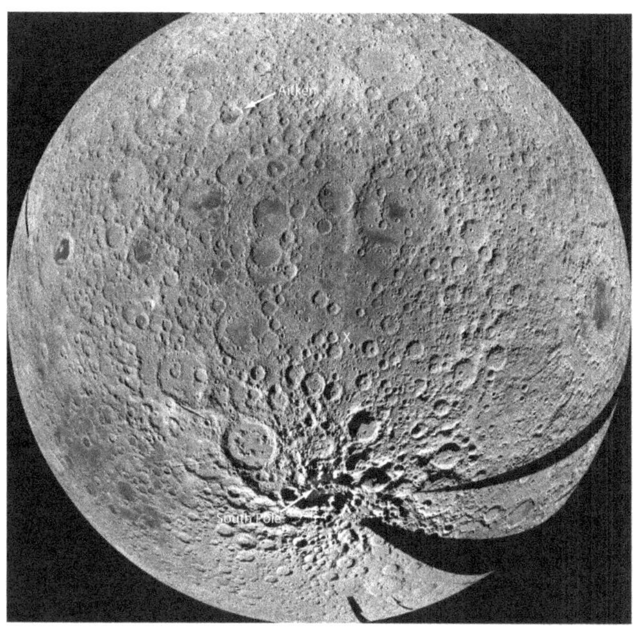

NASA

The South Pole and Aitken basin on the dark side of the Moon.

program: the Yutu rover landing on the moon in 2013; the ongoing preparations for a moon landing and return with lunar samples; and a moon landing of another rover on the far side of the moon in 2019. Why the far side? The moon has no atmosphere and the far side is relatively protected from noisy radio waves coming from the earth. It is there that the equipment allowing us to access the universe, in the very low frequencies, can be set up. It would open our eyes to the thermal signature of certain radio sources in the Milky Way, to the coherent radio signature of clusters of invisible plasmas in space, and of vast magnetic structures connected to those plasmas.

One of the deepest craters of the solar system, on the far side of the moon, the South Pole of the Aitken basin, 6 km deep, would be the ideal place to study lunar geology and also to carry out experiments on deep cold and vacuums. Along with the just discovered giant 200 meter large cave with 50 km length, these both would be ideal for installing the moon village that the European space agency is working on.

Last but not least, Rosatom, the Russian space agency and NASA are both progressing on the question of reducing the time of space travel through nuclear propulsion. Rosatom will test a system in 2018 and NASA says it is working on a prototype that could reach Mars in only 39 days. The team led by Dr Michael Paluszsek at Princeton Satellite Systems is in the test phase of a promising prototype in fusion propulsion, and needs $20 million to make more progress.

III. Ongoing Win-Win Cooperation and the Potential for Much More

Financing Franco-Chinese projects in France or third countries.

Karel Vereycken

Karel Vereycken, Director of Publication of *Nouvelle Solidarité* took up the very practical question of win-win financing, going through some basic information and posing the challenge for France.

Globalization has massively increased Foreign Direct Investment (FDI).

Karel Vereycken

Long term financing can be carried out by sovereign funds. Sovereign funds are expected to represent 15% of total global assets by 2020, nearly $15 trillion, and be run by 140 sovereign funds, i.e. managed and/or state owned.

What attitude should nations take towards FDIs? Total protectionism or an "open bar"? Neither, the third option is to determine the rules of a true win/win system.

How to work with sovereign funds? France has taken several initiatives in this direction. The most interesting was the creation, in 2014, by the French sovereign fund CDC (Caisse de Depots et de Consignations), which holds $400 billion in total assets, of "CDC International Capital" (CDC-IC). This created new types of instruments, "sovereign counterpart funds." The idea is to match foreign investment with local investment, each contributing equal parts. CDC-IC manages partnerships with the Qatar Investment Authority (QIA), Mubadala, Kingdom Holding Company, China Investment Corporation, Korean Investment Corporation, Russian investment fund, and others.

Some examples: in 2015: CDC-IC and the China Investment Corporation (CIC) jointly invested 2 billion Euros in the Greater Paris project. In late 2017, a tripartite fund of sovereign funds, from Russia, Bahrain and

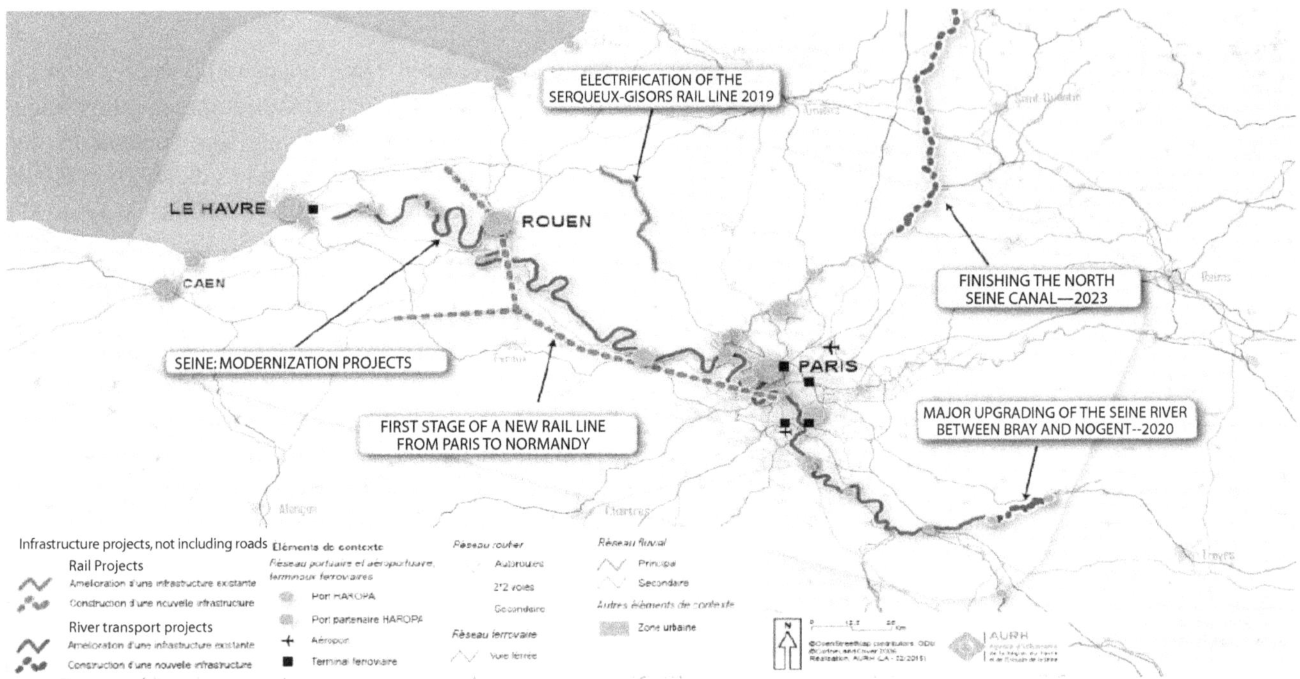

Graphic showing the improvements of existing infrastructure and construction of new infrastructure to greatly expand the French economy by improving the contribution made by the port at Le Havre.

France, saved the famous French glass and crystal manufacturer and distributer, Arc International.

In November 2016, the "Sino-French Third-Countries Investment Fund" which includes Franco-Chinese partnerships in Africa, was created initially with only 300 million Euros, but aims to grow to 2 billion. CDC-IC, without a new policy of sovereign state credit in France, cannot come up with the amounts proposed by China for co-investment. China initially proposed 50 billion Euros, but CDC-IC only had 300 million Euros available.

Vereycken proposed similar investments in infrastructure in France where underinvestment in transport and energy requires at least 250 billion Euros. The urgent needs should start with joint investment with China to improve port infrastructure (dredging, building docks and locks) and building out to the hinterlands (rail and canals). Le Havre, for instance is France's second port and first container port. But 89% of all containers arriving by ship are then forwarded by road, a much higher proportion than in Antwerp, Rotterdam or Hamburg. Paradoxically, Alsace-Lorraine, because of its proximity to Antwerp, Rotterdam and Hamburg, has better maritime access than Bretagne or Southern France on the Mediterranean. The port of Le Havre is still missing the lock connection of the container port with the inland canal network, which is of the utmost urgency. Separating cargo rail from passenger trains between Le Havre, Rouen, and Paris, and all the way to Germany is also a major challenge. At least 2.5 billion Euros are immediately necessary to avoid a total breakdown. Building a high speed rail, maglev or aérotrain connection between Paris, Rouen, and Le Havre would allow the conversion of the current railway grid to good transport. Conclusion: a good framework of mutual confidence exists, therefore let's use it and go ahead with it, Vereycken concluded.

Industrialization in Africa under way!

Sebastien Perimony

Sebastien Perimony, of the Schiller Institute Africa desk in France, attacked the totally false image of Africa, always poor and backwards, never civilized, which has neither history nor heroes! Not only is this image, presented by some French officials, false, but with the emergence of the 

Sebastien Perimony

BRICS and of the China's One Belt, One Road initiative, Africa has entered into an era of co-development,

An overpass on the high-speed rail link between the Kenyan port of Mombasa and Kenyan capital Nairobi, built in collaboration with China.

bringing not only colonization but the bad joke called "development aid" to an end.

A new world is opening up for Africa, as the June 2017, 78-page report by the McKinsey Company, "Dance of the lions and the dragons" reviews. Since the beginning of the millennium, trade between Africa and China has increased by close to 20% each year, and foreign direct investments grew annually during the last decade by 40%. In 2015, China invested $21 billion in African infrastructure and overall investments in infrastructure grew by a 16% annual rate, between 2012 and 2015.

Some examples

Nigeria : On July 2016, Nigeria inaugurated the first high-speed rail line in Western Africa, linking the capital Abuja to Kaduna, 187 km away, at 150 km/h, three times faster than other trains. This line was built by the China Engineering Construction Company (CCECC) and aims at enhancing the economy of Northern Nigeria, which is suffering from the expansion of the Boko Haram cult. Everybody knows that it is economic hardship that pushes youth into the arms of the terrorists and the only solution to that problem is economic development in the region.

The Nigerian government and China's rail giant, China Railway Construction Corporation (CRCC), also signed a $12 billion contract for the construction of a 1,402 km rail line connecting Lagos, Nigeria's capital, to Calabar in the East of the country, and passing through Harcourt Port and the Warri petrochemical factory. 200,000 people will be employed to complete a project which will employ 30,000 permanently. Ethiopia: The first high-speed rail line in Ethiopia was inaugurated on October 2016. The new 753 km rail line will reduce the time of the Djibouti-Addis-Ababa trip to only 10 hours, as opposed to 7 days previously. On Sept. 14, 2014 the six lane highway connecting Addis-Ababa to Adame, 85 km away was opened. Owned by a public company, the highway was built by China Communications Construction Company (CCCC). This new dynamic has created the conditions for the number of children attending school to double in 10 years, and, during the same period, 30 new universities have been created, and the number of students in higher education has gone from 3,000 to 37,000. Electrical power increased from 350 MW to 2,400 MW and 6,000 new MW will be added to the power grid in 2018 when the Ethiopian Renaissance great dam will be inaugurated. The railway network is also in full expansion, slated to increase from 800 km at present, to 4,000 km in the near future. Also of note, Ethiopia, with the help of China, just concluded construction of its first metro line, the first metro line in sub-Saharan Africa, connecting the airport to the city of Addis Ababa. Sixty thousand passengers per day are expected to take this metro soon.

Kenya: Kenya just inaugurated its first high-speed rail line connecting its capital Nairobi to Mombasa, its port on the Indian Ocean, 472 km away. Ninety percent financed by China's EximBank, the total cost was $3.8 billion. This is the first large infrastructure project carried out by Kenya since its independence in 1963! Completed in the record time of 2.5 years, the project employed 46,000 workers which included eight female conductors trained in Beijing. The project generated 1.5% of the economic growth of the country.

Transaqua is the best solution to develop our continent

Mana Boubabakari

Mana Boubabakari, the technical director of the "Lake Chad Basin Commission" (LCBC), gave a short but pointed outline of the current efforts to restore Lake Chad to re-establish the former level of Lake Chad and other wetlands through water transfer. The plan is to reverse

Mana Boubabakari

the degradation of the ecosystem and establish the integrated management of water resources.

A masterplan to save Lake Chad and its environment was initially made at the 6th Summit of the Head of States and Government of the LCBC in N'Djamena on Oct. 28-29, 1987.

The earlier plan, the Transaqua project, developed by the Italian engineering firm Bonifica after the 1973 Sahel drought, was considered as diplomatically too complex and expensive in 1987, so the LCBC member states restricted themselves to considering the smaller alternative called the Ubangi-Lake Chad Water Transfer.

Now, Transaqua is back on the table. The project is technically and environmentally feasible, economically viable and crucial to reducing and eventually eliminating the current exodus of populations fleeing poverty and terrorism.

Transaqua will capture 100 billion of the Congo River's 1.9 trillion cubic meters of water—five percent of the water that flows untapped into the Atlantic Ocean each year. It means building a 2,400-km navigable canal east of the Congo River, northwest across the Democratic Republic of Congo (DRC) to the Cen-

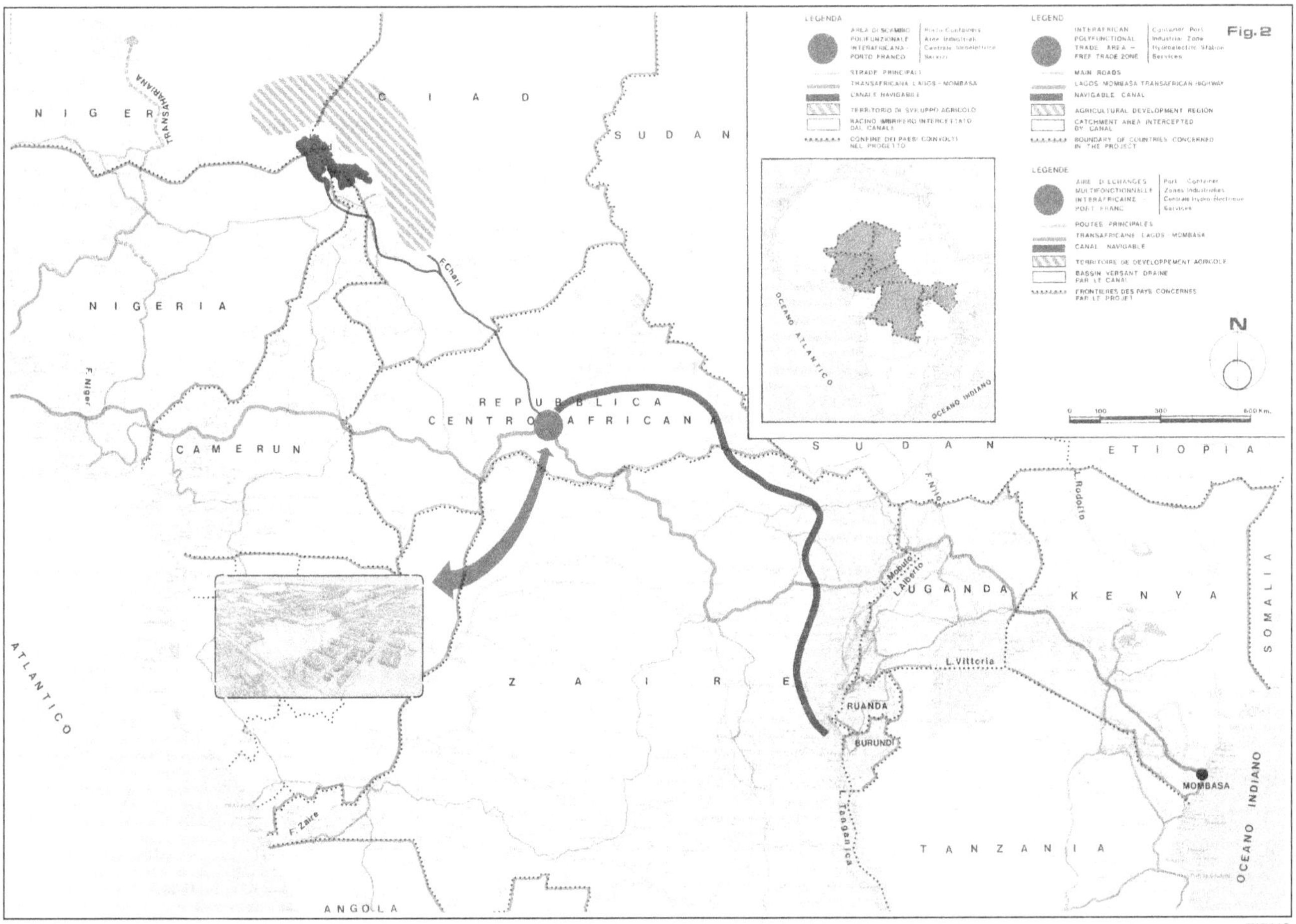

The proposed Transaqua water transfer project from the Democratic Republic of Congo to Lake Chad.

tral African Republic (CAR) connecting to the Chari River.

The project will generate up to 30-35 billion kWh of hydroelectricity through the mass movement of water by gravity; expand a series of irrigated areas for crops or livestock over an area of 5-7 million hectares in the Sahel zone in Chad, north-east Nigeria, northern Cameroon and Niger. Transaqua will also intersect the Lagos-Mombasa Trans-African Highway (ports, river-roads goods distribution)

While Transaqua will transfer 3,200 cubic meters per second, the smaller Ubangi Water Transfer would only transfer 320 cubic meters. The latter could only raise the level of Lake Chad by 1 m compared with up to 5 m by Transaqua. Transaqua is a global infrastructure platform which will bring not only agricultural, demographic and industrial prosperity but also security, and education to at least 12 nations.

The good news is that an agreement was signed with Power China to study the best solutions. Also a convention between Power China and Bonifica will make sure that all the accumulated knowledge will not be lost. Things from here on are on the move and the international conference on saving Lake Chad in April 2018 should mark the beginning of a new era.

The New Silk Road will reconstruct war-torn Middle East countries

Michel Raimbaud

French Ambassador Michel Raimbaud: OBOR (One Belt, One Road), so different than the "bomber democracy" of the West!

Former French ambassador to Mauritania, Sudan and Zimbabwe, and former director of the French "Office for the Protection of Refuges and Stateless Persons" (OFPRA), Michel

French Ambassador Michel Raimbaud

Raimbaud, is known as a relentless critic of all brands of imperialism.

For him, China's Belt and Road initiative definitely creates "a lot of trouble for the Anglo-Saxon geopoliticians" for whom those controlling what Mackinder branded the "Heartland" (Eurasia) would control the oceans, and therefore the world. Today, China's New Silk Road policy also means a new era for the "Muslim Green Belt," while the neo-conservatives' "democratization projects" were a means to destroy those nations through atomization.

Beijing, according to Raimbaud, is no longer ashamed of its geo-economical ambitions: securitize its energy and raw material supplies by a "federative project" bolstering its economic influence in the 64 countries stretching from Eurasia to the African continent.

However, he added, it has to be underscored that "OBOR, is based on the constructive logic of cooperation diametrically opposed to the military and destructive approach adopted by the Unites States over the last quarter century."

OBOR reaches 4.4 billion people, nearly 2/3 of the world population, comprised of 900 projects and $900 billion in investments, the equivalent of four times the Marshall Plan. By its geographic and financial scope, it cannot but attract the 16 countries of the Middle East and Northern Africa which make up the Silk Road Economic Belt and the resurrection of the ancient trade routes connecting Bahrain, Egypt, Iran, Iraq, Israel, Lebanon, Jordan, Kuwait, Oman, Palestine, Qatar, Saudi Arabia, Syria, Turkey, the UAE, and Yemen." OBOR has nothing to do with George W. Bush's "Greater Middle East," a plan to conquer and break up the region, not the "win-win" policy of China, but the "lose-lose" policies of the neo-cons.

Raimbaud, praising the Schiller Institute's program for the reconstruction of Syria and the World Land Bridge, described in great detail how three major countries, namely Iran, Syria and Lebanon have an established interest to see one of the three major economic corridors connecting China, Central Asia and South-East Asia reopened, as well as the return of the Maritime Silk roads. OBOR offers a different future than the "bomber democracy" of the West.

"Admittedly, the New Silk Road is a Chinese project, conceived, financed and applied under Chinese direction. OBOR is conceived as an instrument of influence, not as an instrument of charity, but it offers these three countries the perspective of stability, respectful cooperation and insurance against extremism and the threat of terrorism. It rebuilds their future."

Yemen, from Felix Arabia To Crimes of War

Paul Bonnenfant

Paul Bonnenfant, former researcher at the Institute for Research and Study of the Arab and Muslim World, a project of France's CNRS (National Center for Scientific Research), then spoke about Yemen, a country which was an important part of China's Silk Road for many centuries and which is today being destroyed by a Saudi Coalition supported and armed by the Western powers.

Paul Bonnenfant

After outlining the strategic reasons pushing the Saudis to do this, he described the terrible situation: 9,000 dead, 49,000 wounded, 3 million displaced—all the result of this war. Seventeen million Yemenites are suffering food insecurity (two-thirds of the population) of which seven million are threatened by famine. Four hundred-sixty thousand children need urgent food aid. According to the WHO, there could be 600,000 cases of cholera by end of 2017: The entire country has been affected, but cholera is highest in areas of the worst malnutrition. The main cause is lack of hygiene, lack of water, and the collapse of the health system. Saudi Arabia has systematically targeted water reservoirs, pumping installations, hospitals, and health centers. Bonnenfant went through the heavy destruction of the cultural patrimony including religious centers, ancient buildings, and manuscripts.

"Saudi Arabia and its allies are guilty of war crimes in Yemen," he reported. While the Houthis have engaged in violations of human rights, "it is the Saudi led coalition which is the primary culprit accused by the NGOs."

What can France do? Be coherent with its signing of "The Arms Trade Treaty" governing international weapons trade adopted in 2014 by the UN to which "France declares solemnly to attach the greatest importance."

Bonnenfant continued, "Those beautiful intentions and French declarations are totally contradicted by the facts. … the very official Report to the Parliament on the weapons sales by France in 2015, speaks of 'economic success' … a historic success which made of France the number two world exporter of weapons in 2015, a year during which France registered 16 billion Euros in contracts, of which three-fourths were orders destined for the Middle East."

"I deplore that in March 2016, President Hollande presented the Saudi Interior minister, Mohammed bin Nayef with the Legion of Honor medal, an honor perhaps for that Prince, but no honor to the Legion of Honor." The fact is that "civilians in Yemen are under the fire of the Leclerc tanks and the Mirage 2000s, which France sold respectively to the United Arab Emirates and to Qatar in preceding years. Saudi Arabia, the leader of the Coalition, was the number one client of France from 2009 to 2015. One can say, with no risk of being wrong, that a good part of those bombs, shells, and missiles which are harassing, killing, and wounding the Yemenite people and destroying their patrimony, are of French origin. That's the precise point which depends on France, that is, on us."

Destroyed house in the south of Sana'a, Yemen, Dec. 6, 2015.

cc/Ibrahem Qasim

Creativity, R&D, Infrastructure, from Hamilton, Carey, and List, to LaRouche

Jacques Cheminade

Jacques Cheminade

Jacques Cheminade, economist and former candidate for President of France, presented a closing strategic report. He began, "It was in 1964, after France had recognized, on January 27, the People's Republic of China and established diplomatic relations, that General de Gaulle declared, 'It is not excluded that China becomes once again during the next century, what it was throughout the centuries, the greatest power of the Universe.'" Not because he appreciated Mao Zedong, but because he had a clear view into the future.

The prophetic words of de Gaulle have not yet been fully realized. But the road has been laid out as presented by Xi Jinping at the 19th Party Congress.

This ongoing transformation is in unprecedented in history, considering the number of people involved, and is due to two fundamental elements. First of all, China did not do what we did, in particular after 1971. The adoption by the Western countries of the British system of political economy had disastrous consequences; it was submission to a monetarist conception of the economy, defined by monetary profit. The most extreme element was the decision by the European Union to demand that member states include the revenues of drugs and of other illicit traffic in determining their GDP figures.

In that system, misappropriated credit is an instrument to maintain short and medium term financial indebtedness, in the least worst case to sustain consumption, and for the worst, to inflate the overblown financial bubble for financial gaming. Financial credit institutions acting in this way have, in fact, taken control of the nation states. You see at the Eurogroup, representatives of the IMF, of the ECB and of the European Commission speak before anyone else—the ministers or heads of states of the different countries, end up reduced to the role of yes men in paper straight-jackets. It is a well-known fact in the United States that, other than military spending, or spending associated with that sector, there has been no major investment in the last 50 years.

In direct contrast to that suicidal conception which always sacrifices long term interests, China chose a credit policy in favor of infrastructure, long term investments and low interest rates. True, $20 trillion in debt has accumulated in ten years, but $10 trillion have been invested in infrastructure. If we take as point of reference the total factor of productivity, an index measuring the impact of advanced technologies on physical productivity of labor, we see in the United States of Franklin Roosevelt productivity of 3 to 3.5%; and of same order in France

Charles de Gaulle

Alexander Hamilton

Mathew Carey

Henry Carey

Friedrich List

and Germany and Europe starting in 1950, and 3.11% in China between 1999 and 2011 according to U.S. economic statistics.

China has adopted the economic conception of public productive credit and of investments in infrastructure. These were the American policies of Alexander Hamilton, Mathew and Henry Carey, and the "American System" of Henry Clay. This conception was also presented by Friedrich List in his "National System of Economic Policy," which is very well-known and appreciated in China, as is "indicative planning," a French conception which China has adopted, while we in France have abandoned it.

The secret of the unprecedented development of China, on the one hand, is to be found in the qualities of the Chinese people, as was earlier said here, and in its own past industrial experience, through the Tang and the Song.

Xinhua

Chinese astronaut Zhai Zhigang waves to the camera as he conducts China's first spacewalk, in this video grab taken on September 27, 2008.

These are the Confucian qualities which have been re-adopted today but these qualities are also an adoption of the principles which allowed the development of our own western economies, when they were still developing.

What are those principles? First, start from the fact that human creativity is the source and measure of the real economy, not financial profit expressed in monetary terms. The aim of economics is to create the most favorable conditions for the development of the creative capacities of human individuals at both the national level and in all other nations.

Secondly, concretely, it means putting a stop to the protection of financial speculation. That's what Roosevelt applied under the name of Glass Steagall, or banking separation in the United States.

China has a system which is approximately equivalent to Glass Steagall, with the same impact; commercial banks have public support but not investments banks. True, China has non-banks which correspond to our speculative funds, but there, the whole system controls or can control the situation. This is the reason why in China, two-thirds of the credit allocated to the non-financial sector is concentrated in 22 large companies, which are focused on infrastructure and energy.

Thirdly, there is choosing investment-worthy projects and how to ensure the competence of those who lead them. The criteria established by Friedrich List, by Mathew and Henry Carey, and by advisors to Sergei Witte in Russia, and even more, by our economic plan-

ners after the war, is that of a bet on the future, the bet in France, after the war, on our indicative planning, and that of the KfW in Germany and the criteria of those bets, are the intensity of capital investments, i.e. physical capital—generally speaking the machines and the human capital, oriented towards a maximization of production and the principle of least action, i.e. a maximization of the free energy produced, relative to the energy used by the system: The increase, then, of the energy flux density and of technologies. Physical production with a constant increase per capita, per unit of surface and unit of matter used by the system, with the objective of long term investment, or as the Chinese call it, "patient capital." Lastly: the improvement of the quality of human labor, training and education to ever higher levels in order to organize higher platforms of the system.

Those three fundamental orientations cannot express themselves concretely except on two conditions. The first is their inter-connectivity: between investment in infrastructure, in energy, in transports and in services associated with them, and then with the school system, the health system and in research, with a transformation principle being the common denominator in everything.

The second, more important, is the improvement of the quality of labor. Investment must go to fundamental discoveries, their technological applications and the innovation of those applications. China has thus gone from innovation to technological applications and is at this point at the level of fundamental discoveries. It's a dynamic whole: education of labor from school age and

China's Experimental Advanced Superconducting Tokamak (EAST).

continuing throughout life, and the great projects—space, nuclear energy, advanced technologies in sectors which can generate an environment of research and of increase in the density of technologies in use and the criteria that must define that choice. It is there where human creation expresses itself, where investments must be made.

The question is not to create "Homo Deus", who masters NBIC technologies (Nano, Bio, Info, Cognitive), technologies—technologies which are essential, if they are associated with the transformation of the physical economy, but which can, however, become (in the logic of "homo deus"), and this is happening in front of our eyes, disastrous, if these technologies are seen as things in themselves. Clearly, in and by themselves, information technologies have not led to any increase in real productivity.

Robert Gordon, in the "Rise and Fall of American Growth" demonstrates this well. This means, to be even more clear, that in order to go to space, you have to have propulsion by the highest technologies, i.e. thermonuclear controlled fusion with the contribution of robotics and digital technologies in order to manage and control processes that go beyond human sense-perception. It's that combination that allows us to go towards the future.

Lyndon LaRouche has gone further than taking into account these principles, by establishing the unified criterion underlying the global dynamic of progress. This is his Potential Relative Population Density of society. Relative means the increase in the supporting capacity made possible by the introduction of constant new fundamental discoveries in the form of new technologies applying discoveries of those new physical principles. The Russian scientist and expert in the physical economy of space travel, Pobisk Kuznetsov, baptized that principle, with the name of the "La" principle and many Russian universities speak about this concept, while the ignorance in the West is total concerning this contribution.

Today, this perspective is expressed in what our American colleagues call Lyndon LaRouche's Four Laws. Strict Banking separation, Glass Steagall, to bring Wall Street and its speculations to an end, a policy of productive public credit to relaunch the economy through real development, a true national bank, not a central bank under the control of private speculative financial forces—as are the Federal Reserve and the European central bank—and investment in the highest energy flux density, i.e. in the energy which we know today as thermonuclear controlled fusion and which tomorrow could be matter/antimatter.

Let's now take Xi Jinping's terms, as he expressed them with his economic advisors: a win-win system founded on mutual advantage, investment in infrastructure and in the most advanced technologies, "patient capital," i.e. long term, in a society which is innovative in principle, and finally an inclusive interconnected system in each element of this dynamic.

Let us say it bluntly. The question is not to globalize or to de-globalize. We must recognize that for 25 years international relations, since the fall of the Berlin Wall, were wasted and that those wrong policies are leading us today to financial chaos, to the war of all against all and that this will lead us to armed conflict if we don't change the direction.

China and the BRICS offer us the possibility for change, a change of paradigm as Mrs. LaRouche called it, and of which I have tried to develop the underlying principles. This means we have to rediscover our true selves, come back to the best part of our historic contribution. It is a question of will, of what the Americans call leadership at a moment of great crisis, having the courage to confront the financial dictatorship, wrongly called liberalism.

Let us bet therefore on peace. I think this is the commitment we must make today.

PHILOSOPHICAL PRINCIPLES OF THE COMING EURASIAN WORLD

LaRouche's 'Platform of a Planetary Culture'

The following is an edited transcript of a presentation given by EIR *Editorial Board Member William F. Wertz, Jr., to the LaRouche PAC Manhattan meeting on Saturday, Oct. 28, 2017. Due to the length of the discussion, the question and answer session has been omitted. A video of the full dialogue is available.*

We are at what Friedrich Schiller (1759-1805) would call a *punctum saliens* in world history. We are in the midst of an ongoing attempted coup against the President of the United States by the British Empire. Already the first indictments have been handed down by special counsel Robert Mueller, and more are expected. This is a very hot situation, and it occurs just as President Trump is leaving for Asia, where he'll be going to Japan, South Korea, Vietnam and the Philippines, and most important to China, where he'll be meeting with President Xi. This is a trip that could and must change the world. As we have been advocating for some time, it's crucial that the United States, if it is to rediscover itself as a force for good in the world, join with China, and with Russia and India, in the Eurasian Land-Bridge, a grand design which ironically was first conceptualized by Lyndon LaRouche and Helga Zepp-LaRouche long before China officially adopted it under President Xi in 2013.

In moments like this, it's important to step back and look at the principles which must underlie such a grand design involving major nations, and in some cases, major civilizations, as with China. In 2004, Lyndon LaRouche wrote a document called "The Coming Eurasian World." Prior to this, the LaRouche movement had advocated a Eurasian Land-Bridge and eventually a World Land-Bridge. However, in this document, what LaRouche lays out is the basis for a treaty agreement between Europe and Asia, based on principles. He argues that unless it's based on philosophical principles, it will not necessarily be an agreement which is going to last or can be trusted. He refers to this agreement as a Second Treaty of Westphalia.

The Treaty of Westphalia was the treaty which

The Ratification of the Treaty of Münster (Westphalia) by Gerard Terborch, 1648.

ended the Thirty Years' religious war in Europe in the year 1648. The key conception in it was the respect for national sovereignty—that is, the principle of self-determination—and also the concept that the relations among sovereign nation-states should be based upon the principle of the "advantage of the other." This is a very fundamental concept which is something shared by all of humanity, no matter which culture, no matter which religion. The idea is that what the Greeks call *agapē*, or love, should be the basis of all foreign policy.

Today, there are many who are critical of China. But look at what China is doing in the world; look at what it has done for its own people. China has lifted something in the range of 700 million people out of poverty over the recent decades. In the recent party congress in Beijing, a commitment was made to lift the remaining 42 million Chinese poor out of poverty. but they are not only concerned about the general welfare of their own population; they are committed to the same policy for the rest of humanity.

The policy of the Chinese government is "the advantage of the other." It's a commitment to the General Welfare. I think it's safe to say that China, which is a Confucian country, is actually acting in a more Christian way than Western Europe and the United States. There are many critics of China—including this fellow who was in the Trump administration and has since left, Steve Bannon. But you have to look at what China is doing; and then look at what we—who have in large part abandoned the principles which were the basis of the founding of the United States of America in the first place—are doing, or not doing. We are not even taking care of our own population. We haven't been for decades. And we have certainly not committed ourselves to a worldwide policy, which was the policy of Franklin Roosevelt before he died. As reported by his son Elliott Roosevelt, Franklin Roosevelt had told Winston Churchill that the United States was not fighting World War II to preserve the British Empire, but rather that after the war we intended to use American System methods to develop the rest of the world and to eliminate colonialism.

Proceeding from a 'Higher Vantage Point'

Unfortunately, with the exception of Lyndon LaRouche, who has fought for Roosevelt's policy perspective throughout his entire life, that has not been the policy of the United States over the decades which have elapsed since Roosevelt's death, even though there have been those who have fought a rear-guard effort, such as John F Kennedy, to pursue that Roosevelt policy.

In his work, "The Coming Eurasian World," LaRouche says, "If the U.S.A. is to resume a long-neglected useful function for the world at large, a mission orientation which the U.S. would have adopted at the close of the last great war, but for the untimely death of President Franklin Roosevelt, we must now take into account the pressing needs of the population of regions such as Asia for a chiefly postponed, rapid influence of technological improvements in both the circumstances of life and means of production to lift the masses of Asia, within not less than two generations up to a truly self-sustaining level."

He continues: "My approach is to proceed from a higher vantage point than either European or Asian culture. To stand on the platform of what I foresee as the emergence of a specifically Eurasian culture, a planetary culture." Then he goes on to say, "We must present Asian leaders with a view on the interrelated subjects of monotheism and Promethean man. The entirety of European civilization is a struggle to bring about the establishment of a sovereign nation-state republic which replaces the anti-human heritage of evil oligarchy typified by the Olympian Zeus." The point that he further makes is that Asian nations like China and India, in particular, have been subjected precisely to the policies of the Olympian Zeus in the form of the British Empire. Look at what happened to India under the British Empire; look at what happened to China during the mid 19th-century British Opium Wars. And look at what has happened to Russia as a result of the geopolitical policies of the British Empire.

Now, what LaRouche continues to say is that what the Asian intellectual must do is look at the struggle which has occurred in Western civilization. And he goes back to the period of Solon in Athens and Lycurgus in Sparta. I would refer people to Friedrich Schiller's essay on the "Legislation of Lycurgus and Solon," because the contrast between these two societies represents the struggle which has occurred within Western civilization, and has not yet been fully won to this day. Let me read from Schiller's writing on this. He says, "The state itself is never the purpose, it is important only as the condition under which the purpose of mankind may be fulfilled, and this purpose of mankind is none other than the development of all the powers of people, i.e., progress. If the constitution of a state hin-

Solon

Lycurgus

ders the progress of the mind, it is contemptible and harmful.... Laws are contemptible and harmful if they constrain a power of the human mind, if they impose upon the mind any sort of stagnation."

In the case of Lycurgus of Sparta, he said, "He worked against the highest purpose of humanity, in that, through his well thought-out system of state, he held the minds of the Spartans fast at the level where he had found them, and hemmed in all progress for eternity.

"All industry was banned, all science neglected, all trade with foreign peoples forbidden ... The Spartan state was intended to revolve solely around itself, in perpetual uniformity, in a sad egoism."

"Progress of mind should be the purpose of the state. Lycurgus's state could persist under but one condition, that the mind of the people stagnates, and he was thus only able to sustain his state by trespassing against the highest and only purpose of the state."

In contrast to Lycurgus, Schiller points out that the first edict of Solon upon assuming office was to cancel the debt that was oppressing the citizens of Athens. "All debts were annulled, and it was forbidden at the same time, that in the future anyone be permitted to borrow on his own person." And he further writes about Solon, "he had respect for human nature, and never sacrificed people to the state, never the end to the means; rather let the state serve the people." This is the fight that has existed within Western European civilization dating back

to that time, at least, and continuing forward. The fundamental issue is whether the society is organized to promote or to stifle that which distinguishes man from a beast—his creative reason.

This same issue was also central to the fight between the Olympian Zeus and Prometheus in Greek mythology. Zeus wanted to suppress human creativity, keep man in the dark as a means of politically controlling him. What Prometheus did out of his love for humanity, was to give man fire. That is, he gave man science and technology, so that he had a hope for the future.

The Basis for Human Development

As Plato writes in his *Philebus* dialogue, Prometheus also gave man a method of creative scientific thinking. The basic idea, developed explicitly in the *Philebus* dialogue and then much later in human history by Nicholas of Cusa (1401-64), by Georg Cantor (1845-1918), by Bernhard Riemann (1826-66), and by Lyndon LaRouche, is that the created universe is characterized by becoming, by a process of change, which must be ordered by a transfinite process of higher-order hypotheses, which results in a higher order of human productivity, so as to increase the level of potential relative population density, a concept uniquely developed by Lyndon LaRouche.

A simple example: If a society stays in one mode of production, such as burning wood as a source of energy, eventually it will run out of wood, and will deforest the entire area. You then have to go ever further distances to bring the wood back, which increases its social cost. So, does that mean that we have limits to growth, and that resources are finite? That's what the book *Limits to Growth* has argued; that's what you're taught in the schools these days: that there are finite resources, therefore we shouldn't have industry; we shouldn't have a growing population. But the reality is that mankind has progressed by developing a succession of higher order hypotheses, what Cantor called a "transfinite," which defines qualitatively new, more energy-dense modes of production. For example, we discovered the use of coal, which has a greater energy-flux density than wood. We also then moved to the development of fission power, based on uranium. We have the capacity to develop fusion power, which uses helium-3 that you can find on the Moon, as a source of energy. But the basic idea is that through his creative reason and his love of humanity, man can and must make scientific revolutions, upon which basis new technologies can be introduced, which redefine the resource base, so that man can increase his potential relative population density and thus his mastery over the universe.

This is the implication of the conception developed by Plato in the *Philebus* dialogue, where he argues that Prometheus passed on to man the saying that, "All things consist of a one and a many, and have in their nature a conjunction of limit and unlimitedness." If you merely impose "the one," or a limit on "the many" or the unlimited, then you get stagnation. But there's a different conjunction, in which there is an unlimited family of higher-order limits. That's the conception which Plato developed in the *Philebus*, and it's the conception which is the center of progress in humanity.

Lyndon LaRouche argues that there has been an ongoing fight within Western civilization against the imperial, bestial conception of man, which the Roman Empire represented, going back to the period of the foundation of Christianity. True Christianity, for example, under Charlemagne (742-814), fought against this bestial conception. But when human creativity was suppressed in the 1300s by the Venetian Empire, mankind suffered from what became known as the New Dark Age, a period characterized by depopulation due to the Black Death and the Hundred Years' War.

The Council of Florence

The key turning point in this battle was the Council of Florence, which met in Florence, Italy from 1439 to 1444. This Council brought Orthodox Christians from Russia and from Greece, to Florence, to meet with the

Painting by Benozzo Gozzoli

"The Journey of the Magi" (1459), depicts the procession of the patriarchs of the Eastern Orthodox Church to the Council of Florence (1439).

Roman Catholic representatives. Nicholas of Cusa was very instrumental in pulling this meeting together. As a result of this meeting and what it focused on, mankind's power over nature was vastly increased to the benefit of humanity.

The fundamental issue of the Council of Florence is something called—in Latin—the *Filioque*; which means "and the Son." "Filio" means "son," "que" means "and." In the Credo, it is stated that the Holy Spirit proceeds from the Father "and the Son"; that is, the Son of God, Jesus Christ. But by implication, this procession of the Holy Spirit also from the Son applies to all human beings insofar as they imitate the mind of Christ. The basic issue was that the Russian Orthodox and the Greek Orthodox churches did not adhere to the *Filioque* conception; they thought it was an aberration. But at the Council of Florence, what they agreed upon was that this was not an aberration, but a conception coherent with Christianity. They released a proclamation of jubilation because they had reached an agreement which allowed the Church at that time to unify for the first time since the schism of 1054.

What is the significance of the *Filioque*? One of the

things that Lyndon LaRouche argues is that the *Filioque* is the basis for economic science. In *The Science of Christian Economy*, written in 1991, he says, "Economic science was developed, in fact, by Christianity. Furthermore, the evidence is that perhaps economic science could not have been developed except by Christianity. The essence of this connection is expressed by the *Filioque* of the Latin creed." What's involved here is the conception in Christian theology that the Son is the Logos. For instance, if you look at the Gospel of St. John, it begins with "In the beginning was the *logos*." And from there it goes on to stress, "And the *logos* was with God, and the *logos* was God. He was in the beginning with God. All things came through him, and without him nothing came to be." And then later, it says "and the *logos*," or the Word, "became flesh."

So this is the fundamental idea. And the Holy Spirit is *agapē*, the Greek word for love. So, you have a congruence in this idea of the *Filioque* of creative reason—the *logos*—of the universe as embodied in man; and *agapē*, or love. It's this combination that drives economic science on behalf of mankind. That combination of agapic creative reason is uniquely the capability of human beings. This was realized by those like Nicholas of Cusa and his associates in this period of the Council of Florence.

Man's Power in the Universe

In an article titled, "A Philosophy for Victory: Can We Change the Universe?" written Feb. 11, 2001, Lyndon LaRouche makes the following point: "Classical philosophy, properly defined, is the only branch of science in which possible solutions to a crisis can be rationally discussed. Man is a creature distinguished from the beasts by his free will, which is otherwise called Reason or natural law. Man's free will coheres with a universal principle of physical economy—anti-entropy; the human noetic will." "Noesis" is the Greek word for creative reason, and "the will" is the love, the passion required to take action on the basis of creative reason. Since the human mind is capable of infinite concept formation, this capability is anti-entropic and defines man's capacity to overcome all limits to growth.

Human progress occurs when you have societies which foster this quality. When in the spirit of Zeus this quality is denied, as has been the case in Western European civilization over the post-World War II period, and

Cardinal Nicholas of Cusa

even going back further, going back to Bertrand Russell—to the beginning of the 1900s—stagnation or worse occurs. Instead of creative reason, what is emphasized is empiricism and logical deduction. There is nothing which distinguishes man from a beast from the standpoint of empiricism, in which you just know what you perceive with your senses, or from the standpoint of logical deduction, where you can only come to conclusions based on fixed categories of thought, which categories of thought are the very reason for your self-destruction.

This is the reason we have not had the fundamental breakthroughs in science and art that we had in the 1800s. Where is the Bernhard Riemann? Where is the Gauss? Where is the Kepler? Where is the Beethoven? Why is it we cannot produce Classical music today on a level which goes one step higher than the highest peak achieved previously? Such progress occurred in rapid succession in an earlier period, when we had Bach, we had Mozart, we had Beethoven, and others following Beethoven. We've lost that capability. That quality of agapic creative reason, however, is the crucial determining factor in man's power over nature as expressed in the true current of Christianity, coming out of the Council of Florence. At that point, we also had further developments. We had the development of the sovereign nation-state which didn't exist anywhere in the world before then. This was expressed in a book called *Concordantia Catholica* or *Universal Concordance* by Nicholas of Cusa. There he developed the concept of national sovereignty. He also developed the idea that peace could only be achieved if all people elevate their minds to the level at which they are in rational or intellectual harmony with the *logos* of the universe.

The basic idea, which is also expressed in the work of Vladimir Vernadsky (1863-1945), the Russian scientist, whom Lyndon LaRouche refers to particularly in his essay on "Earth's Next Fifty Years," is that man, if he is creative, is a *geological* force. Look at the power of nature; it's nothing compared to what man is capable of doing to the extent to which he is acting in a creative and *agapic* manner.

In "A Philosophy for Victory; Can We Change the Universe?" Lyndon LaRouche writes: "It is the willful action of the individual human mind in making a valid discovery of a pre-existing universal principle in the universe which, by willfully applying that same principle, changes the universe from which that discovery had been adduced. It is as if to say that 'In the beginning, was the *logos*.'" So, there's a pre-existing principle of the universe. Man, because he's made in the living image of the Creator, is capable of adducing a scientific breakthrough based on a pre-existing scientific universal principle of creation, and then applying that to the universe, which gives man greater power over nature for mankind's benefit. That's the central conception.

Following the Council of Florence, we had the development of the first nation-states. We had the development of the nation-state in France under Louis XI (1423-83); somewhat later, the development of a nation-state in England under Henry VII (1457-1509). One of the other critical individuals in human history in this whole period, was Joan of Arc (1412-31), who fought the British at that time—the Normans—and was burned at the stake for her efforts. What she was fighting for, was the idea of the nation-state. Friedrich Schil-

Statue of Joan of Arc by Félix Charpentier (1888) before the Sainte-Jeanne-d'Arc Basilica, Paris.

ler wrote a play dedicated to her effort, which ends with the words: "The pain is brief, but the joy shall be eterne." That really captures Schiller's conception of the sublime. The same conception is also manifested in the sacred music of Western Classical music, whether that be "Christ on the Mount of Olives" (of Beethoven) or the Passions of St. Matthew and St. John (Bach). If an individual rises to the level of his creative reason and acts on the basis of *agapē*, as Nicholas of Cusa writes in his book *On Learned Ignorance*, "then with the power of Jesus with whom he is united, he commands even the evil spirits and has power over nature and motion." That's the fundamental scientific conception that the combination of Greek Classical philosophy, particularly Plato, and this current of Christianity has contributed to humanity.

Now, what Lyndon LaRouche makes clear, is the following. He says, "Christianity contains something superior to any other form of culture, objectively speaking, which is not a property of Europe in a strict sense, or of the Americas. What has been contributed by Christian civilization is the rightful property of every person on the surface of the planet." He further writes that this notion of the coextensive congruence of *agapē* and universal acts of creative reason, is "something which is a gift of the Creator, which belongs not to us, but is entrusted to us, to our care as the common property of all mankind."

The obvious irony here is that this principle, this knowledge of what is good about man, and which is critical to the development of a new Treaty of Westphalia on a global scale through Eurasian cooperation, has largely been abandoned by Western Europe. It's not even understood. There are very few people who understand the significance of the *Filioque*, including most of the people who may sit in a mass or attend another religious service and say these words. They don't understand the significance of this conception from an intelligible standpoint. In the face of this ignorance, Lyndon LaRouche makes an ecumenical appeal to people of other religious professions to defend this principle as the common property of all humanity. He writes: "the Jew, the Buddhist, the Muslim must join with us in defense of Christian civilization against the bestialist attempt to destroy Christian civilization with which the British royal household has associated itself."

For this same reason he writes that "Asian patriots must study the history of European civilization more carefully, to see what universal principles are demonstrated, for both European and Asian cultures today, by tracing the internal struggles between right and wrong, in European history, down to the epistemological roots of that conflict."

A New Treaty of Westphalia

One of the key figures who helped to bring about the conceptual basis for the American Revolution was a German by the name of Gottfried Wilhelm Leibniz (1646-1716). Let me read something to you which I think gets at the heart of this conception of the human noetic will, or the congruence of creative reason and *agapē*. He writes in the *Discourse on Metaphysics*: "I hold that to act conformably to the love of God, it is not sufficient to force oneself to be patient; we must be really satisfied with all that comes to us according to his will. I mean this acquiescence in regard to the past; for as regards the future one should not be a quietist with the arms folded, open to ridicule, awaiting that which God will do. . . . It is necessary to act conformably to the presumptive will of God as far as we are able to judge of it, trying with all our might to contribute to the general welfare." In my mind that goes to the heart of the

Gottfried Wilhelm Leibniz
(1646-1716)

matter: Man as a creative species, created in the living image of the Creator, has responsibility to determine as best he can, the presumptive will of God, and to act on that basis, out of love for truth, out of love for humanity.

Now, this is also a concept which Plato developed. In *The Republic*, Plato has a character called Thrasymachus, who argues that "the advantage of the stronger is just." Contrast that to the Treaty of Westphalia, which says one should act on the basis of the advantage of the other. Thrasymachus expresses precisely the opposite, imperial conception. And of course, what Plato also says in *The Republic*, in contrast to that, is that our "guardian to be," that is a leader, "will also need the quality of having the love of wisdom in his nature," which is the question of philosophy, that Lyndon LaRouche developed as crucial earlier.

Turning to China, China is a Confucian society, and Helga Zepp-LaRouche has emphasized repeatedly that President Xi Jinping is a Confucian man. Now, Leibniz, whom I just mentioned, was very involved in attempting to bring about an ecumenical alliance between China and Europe in his time, also as mediated through Russia. This is what he said, in respect to Confucian ideas: "It is pure Christianity insofar as it renews the natural law inscribed in our hearts. I find this quite excellent and quite in accord with natural theology." And if you look at Confucian ideas, you have a reflection of the Trinity and of the *Filioque* in Christianity. The idea of *Li* is what Leibniz calls "reason, the sovereign substance we revere under the name of God. It is eternal, uncreated, everywhere, and everything is in Him." And then *Li* is also, as he says, "the light of reason in man."

And then finally, you have the conception *Ren*, otherwise pronounced "jen" which is the Chinese conception of benevolence or love, or will, what we call "spirit," the Holy Spirit.

So there is embedded, from the standpoint of natural theology in Confucianism, ideas which are consonant with the conceptions in Christianity, which Lyndon LaRouche has developed and which I've tried to indicate to you today.

So the actual basis, in terms of principle, of a Europe-Asia New Treaty of Westphalia—which is what we're talking about, as Trump is about to go to Asia—is this concept which exists in both cultures, although expressed differently. You have in Confucianism, as Leibniz said, ideas which are pure Christianity, renewing the natural law inscribed in our hearts. And then you have in Christianity this conception of the *Filioque* and its implication in terms of human noetic will and the capacity to develop new creative breakthroughs, which allow man to increase his power over nature on behalf of mankind, and that in an anti-entropic manner. To increase one's power over nature is to create a situation where nature is not depleted but actually developed. And this also goes back to a conception of Nicholas of Cusa, which is that the further perfection of creation is latent, or is enfolded, in the mind of the Creator, and then unfolds over time through man as an instrument; because man is in the living image of the Creator, and has that responsibility.

So the idea here is you've got to bring these two cultures together around this common conception. In the *Science of Christian Economy*, Lyndon LaRouche wrote:

"The essence of good … statecraft is the fostering of … sovereign nation-state republics, … [which] ensure the increase of the potential population densities, [promoting] … the sovereign individual's power of creative reason....

"Such anti-oligarchical sovereign nation-state republics are *almost* perfectly sovereign. This sovereignty is to be subordinated to nothing but … natural law....

"A truly sovereign nation-state republic finds a sense of national identity for each of its citizens, in a general spirit of commitment to the special mission which that republic fulfills on behalf of civilization as a whole.

"What we must establish soon upon this planet, … is a *Concordantia Catholica* [which, translated from Latin is, "a universal concordance"], a family of sovereign nation-state republics, each and all tolerating only one supranational authority, *natural law*.... Yet, it is not sufficient that each, as a sovereign republic, be subject passively to natural law. A right reading of that natural law reveals our obligation to cosponsor certain regional and global cooperative ventures, in addition to our national affairs."

That is the actual expression of *agapē*: A sovereign nation-state exists not just to benefit one's own people, but to benefit all of humanity. I think that gets at this issue that Lyndon LaRouche wrote about in terms of creating a *planetary culture*. That is what we have to do, as a human species, which is not in contradiction with national sovereignty, which was the fundamental principle of the Treaty of Westphalia; but it's a national sovereignty which is not egoistic. It's a national sovereignty which is committed to all humanity—as was Roosevelt. Think about Roosevelt's Good Neighbor policy. Think about Kennedy's Alliance for Progress. What do we have that's been similar to that in the recent period—other than what Lyndon LaRouche and Helga Zepp-LaRouche have advocated?

What Unites All Mankind

In 1453, with the help of the Venetians, the Ottoman Turks took over Constantinople, which was a setback for uniting the Eastern and Western divisions of Christianity; it was also a setback in terms of ecumenical relations with Islam at that time. Nicholas of Cusa wrote a book, a dialogue called *On the Peace of Faith*, and this dialogue had as its purpose the creation of a global ecumenical alliance similar to what Leibniz later attempted in respect to China, Europe and Russia, and what we are on the verge of finally creating today, by bringing together Chinese, Indian, Western European civilization, and other cultures around a planetary commitment to mankind—and beyond the planet.

In this work, Cusa has characters from all cultures, all nations of the world, in dialogue, with Peter and Paul representing Christianity. At a crucial point in the dialogue the Tatar says: "It is proper to keep the commandments of God. But the Jews say they have received their commandments from Moses; the Arabs say they have them from Mohammed; and the Christians from Jesus. And there are perhaps other nations who honor their prophets, through whose hands they assert they have received the divine precepts. Therefore, how shall we arrive at concord?" The Apostle Paul says: "The divine commandments are very brief and are all well-known and common in every nation, for the light that reveals them to us, is created along with the rational soul." So again, you have *agapē* and creative reason united in the

Christ driving the money changers from the Temple, 1635, by Rembrandt Harmenszoon van Rijn, 1606-1669.

soul. "For within us, God says to love Him from Whom we received being, and to do nothing to another except that which we wish done to us. Love is therefore the fulfillment of the law of God, and all laws are reduced to this. It should therefore suffice to establish peace in faith and in the law of love, while the rites are tolerated from this time forth."

That is, you can have differences in religious or other customs or rites, but there's one thing which unites all humanity, which is that we're all created by the Creator, and being in His living image, we have the capacity for *agapē*, and we have the capacity for creative reason. Those are the principles upon which a new Eurasian civilization can and must be built.

The "One Belt, One Road" policy is not a matter of making money. The Chinese are probably going to lose money, because they're going into areas of great need, of great political devastation, and they are going there with the idea of creating peace by uplifting populations and getting different ethnic groups, different religions working together in terms of the common destiny of mankind. So it's not about making money, or making economic deals per se. It is not about geopolitics, because they're not trying to turn people all over the world into either Confucians or Communists; they are just basically acting on behalf of humanity; which is what we should be doing, but which we haven't been

doing, because of this history of geopolitics and the fact that the British Empire is still running most of Europe and also much of the United States, as we've seen with the attempted coup against President Trump.

Think more deeply in terms of the principles, philosophical principles, and you'll realize that agreements that are going to last have to be based upon scientific principles, which reflect the nature of man. This is especially crucial for us to understand, because we need the help of Asians in freeing Western European civilization, including the United States, from the British Empire. Empire is not just something physical, in terms of armies; it's the mode of thinking that's been imposed upon people, the financial oligarchical control which is crucial. That's why Solon's first act was to cancel the debt. In that sense he is the original Christ driving the money-changers out of the Temple, or the original Franklin Roosevelt saying that we have to drive the money changers out of the temple of Wall Street.

These are the ideas which we have to study and dedicate ourselves to. We have to regain our lost selves, and we need the Asians to help us in this fight. But to do so, they in turn have to recognize that the West is not the British Empire, which had oppressed them, and continues to plot against them. As Lyndon LaRouche wrote in *The Coming Eurasian World*, one of the problems in India, and he'd spent a lot of time there,—during World War II and then also afterward in visits there, where he and Helga met with Indira Gandhi a number of times— is "a corrupting softness towards the imperial design, which is embedded in all of the sundry elements of the Fabian schemes associated with the names of H.G. Wells and Bertrand Russell." A similar type of problem exists in China and other areas of Asia. So what they need to know are the principles which are the true basis of power, the positive power, the power for good, of Western civilization, which is very difficult to see especially today.

We need a revival of this way of thinking, this current in the West, and at the same time, we need an appreciation on the part of Asia of this anti-oligarchical Christian current, if we are to succeed. The coherence between Confucianism, in particular, and Christianity, of the type that we've been discussing, that's our critical weapon in this fight.

HELGA ZEPP-LAROUCHE

Great Opportunities on the Eve of President Trump's Asia Tour

This is an edited transcript of a webcast by Helga Zepp-LaRouche. The webcast was broadcast Nov. 2, and can be found at http://newparadigm.schillerinstitute.com/

Harley Schlanger: Hello, I'm Harley Schlanger from the Schiller Institute and I'd like to welcome you to this week's webcast with Helga Zepp-LaRouche. Helga, this has been an extraordinary week of crucial strategic developments, which, as is often the case, have been hidden from most of the people in the West. We can start with the fact that President Trump will be going to Asia in a couple of days, and he has a pivotal Nov. 8 meeting with Chinese President Xi Jinping. President Xi gave a very significant message yesterday, where he said he's looking forward to the opportunity to cooperate with the United States on a "win-win" basis.

There are all sorts of Chinese activities, including Russian Prime Minister Medvedev coming to China, and developments on the Silk Road in Ukraine, Portugal and elsewhere. But also, as you had forecast in one of the earlier webcasts, there's an effort to stop all this from taking place, and we saw that with the intervention by the special counsel—the legal assassin Robert Mueller—with a really fraudulent set of indictments on Monday of this week, of Paul Manafort, Trump's campaign manager (June to August 2016), and his aide Rick Gates; and then a classic British FBI sting operation with George Papadopoulos, a former member of the foreign policy advisory panel to Trump's Presidential campaign. Right on cue, David Gergen, former presidential advisor who served in the Nixon, Ford, Reagan, and Clinton administrations, went on CNN and said President Trump should not go to Asia in the middle of this.

So where do things stand, as we're sitting here today?

Helga Zepp-LaRouche: It is very dramatic and very hopeful. I think both Presidents, Trump and Xi, have signalled ahead of the summit their best intention to make this a breakthrough. President Trump gave an extremely interesting interview to Fox TV's Lou Dobbs, where he said that he expects the relationship between the United States and China to be absolutely great; that China is a great country, and that he has an excellent relationship with President Xi Jinping. And then President Xi, from his side, addressed the advisory board of Tsinghua University's School of Economics and Management in Beijing, composed largely of high-powered American business and financial leaders. He told the board that he is looking "far ahead and aiming high" in the relationship with the United States. Tsinghua University is a very prestigious university, and I think this is a very interesting conception. You can also say it's a "vision"—looking "far ahead and aiming high," and I

EIRNS/Michael Steger

"Presidents, Trump and Xi, have signalled ahead of the summit their best intention to make this a breakthrough." Part of the Beijing skyline is shown here.

Xinhua/Xie Huanchi

China Premier Li Keqiang (R) meets Russian Prime Minister Dmitry Medvedev at the 22nd China-Russia Prime Ministers' Regular Meeting, in Beijing, Oct. 31, 2017.

couldn't help but compare that to the policy approach of German Chancellor Merkel, whose policy is always one of "little steps." She once even said that one can only steer as far ahead as one can see.

That's quite a difference in approach! This comes immediately after the 19th National Congress of the CPC, where Xi Jinping managed to unite the whole party behind his vision of the Belt and Road Initiative (BRI), based on the idea of a community of a shared future of mankind. He said that that is going to be discussed in the meeting with President Trump. Therefore I think that the signs are that the relationship between the two most important countries in the world will turn out to be positive. I'm very, very hopeful.

The Western media are just ridiculous. I monitored in particular the German coverage of what's going on in the United States, and it's as if the FBI were running the German media! Because they only report the one side—the Obama, intelligence community side—and they don't report at all what Trump is actually saying. And of course they don't report anything about his upcoming visit.

So I think people will be in for a surprise, because I think the developments cannot be hidden, and my expectations are very high that they will be very positive.

Schlanger: We also have, as I mentioned at the outset, a very active Chinese engagement in the world. There are developments in Portugal with the Maritime Silk Road, and with Ukraine as a possible transit point into Europe. And also, by the way, an important discussion going on between India and China: What can you tell us about that?

Zepp-LaRouche: I think President Xi Jinping has a grand design to overcome all tensions. The "win-win" concept applies to every single country. You can see that, for example, in the case of Japan, whose Prime Minister Abe is moving closer to working with China and the BRI. And the same goes for India, which until very recently had a border conflict with China in Doklam in Tibet [known as Donglang in China], where they actually had a stand-off between the militaries of both sides. But that has apparently been quite successfully calmed down, and relations between China and India are now much improved.

Russian Prime Minister Medvedev was just in Beijing meeting with President Xi Jinping and Prime Minister Li Keqiang and others, and talking about integrating the New Silk Road, the Belt and Road Initiative, with the Eurasian Economic Union. They even talked about creating a "Silk Road on Ice" by joining efforts for the development of the Arctic. So you have all kinds of efforts to overcome tensions in all kinds of conflicts, and I think there is a grand design behind all of this, which is the idea of moving the entire world community up to a new level of relations among nations, overcoming geopolitics.

This is something most people have not yet even started to think about. This is a revolutionary new concept, of overcoming geopolitics by finding a collaboration in the interest of the other, uniting actually all of mankind. I don't know if it will succeed, because there are important forces who are opposing it, but I think the intention, by China, and by President Xi Jinping, to establish such a new model of relationships, is unquestionably real.

Yet people are sort of brainwashed by the Western media. We find many times in the streets, at our information tables, people telling us, "Oh, but I don't trust the Chinese." I would ask these people just to investigate for a little while, and make themselves more familiar with the Chinese grand design, and not simply buy the media reports against China. Why should people believe the media on China, when they are obviously lying on so many other issues? So I would wish the audience—you—to open your minds and to open your hearts, and find out for yourself. Because I think, what we are witnessing right now is one of the most exceptional changes in human history. If this model of the Chinese succeeds, the danger of war and the danger of the extinction of the human race through the use of thermonuclear weapons, for example, will be overcome forever. And that is definitely something which I think is worth trying to accomplish.

Schlanger: Last week, you mentioned that Jim Umpleby, the CEO of Caterpillar, a company that manufactures heavy machinery used for agriculture and construction, said that he's very optimistic about a U.S. role in the New Silk Road. In an interview published by *The Diplomat,* with a leading establishment figure, someone who is inside the institutions, Joseph Nye, former Dean of Harvard University's Kennedy School of Government, stated that he favors U.S. cooperation with China. What is it that the neo-cons and neo-liberals in the establishment fear so much about U.S.-China cooperation?

Zepp-LaRouche: It is so clear that the Chinese model—which is also reflected in the new banking institutions, such as the Asian Infrastructure Investment Bank (AIIB), the New Development Bank of the BRICS countries, the Silk Road Fund, and many similar institutions—is explicitly oriented towards investment in the real economy. And yet, rather than looking at this emerging system of alternative credit institutions as a savior, as something which may eventually even be the lifeboat when the next financial crash hits—which is about to happen at any moment—the West looks at it as a threat. Because as you can see, the entire Western system, especially as it emerged after the collapse of the Soviet Union, was based on the idea of a unipolar world, based on the "special relationship" of the Anglo-Americans, running the world through financial control of the dollar-denominated system.

Against the Old, Dying System

This system obviously worked for some people very well, because they became richer and richer—I mean, just shamelessly rich billionaires, two-digit billion-aires—while a growing majority of the people became poorer, and the middle class was afraid of being put out on the street. So these billionaires defend that system, because that is the basis of their privilege, that is what their money is attached to. And they look askance at the idea of China promoting a model which is truly devoted to the common good—not only the common good of the Chinese people, but very explicitly investing in people and in countries left behind by the trans-Atlantic financial system.

The Chinese are providing credits for infrastructure, for industrial parks, and for agriculture, and this should be seen as a more attractive model. Rather than saying, OK, let's recognize the fact that the Western model did not work; it led to all kinds of rebellions; it led to the Brexit; it led to Hillary Clinton losing the election; it led to the rise of populist parties in Europe. It's actually contributing to the dissolution of the EU at a rather amazing speed, if you look at Spain, if you look at the situation in other areas such as Eastern Europe, for example, which is clearly turning away from the EU…. So it had all of these side-effects—rather than reflecting upon all this and changing, and maybe adjusting to the new offers, they are determined to oppose it by the old tricks, lies, set-ups and coups, if they can. That is why they have not given up.

It's a small elite, but existing in many countries. Those who are going after Trump in the United States, are definitely determined not to let that new system emerge, and we have in Europe, unfortunately, similarly minded people. But they are in trouble, in my view.

Schlanger: Let's turn our attention for a moment to the latest developments in the United States on this: In particular, I want to focus on this plea agreement with this character Papadopoulos, which was based on the fact that they say he lied to the FBI. What did he lie about? Supposedly he was told that the Russians had hacked emails; supposedly he met with a Russian professor—who turns out to be from Malta—and the Russian professor introduced him to Putin's niece—who turned out not to be Putin's niece—and the whole story just reeks of a classic FBI-British sting operation.

Now, you reminded people yesterday, I think it was, that your husband once said that when you're in a battle like this, you can't just counterpunch—and of course Trump is a fairly effective counterpuncher—but you have to outflank the enemy. How could he do that?

LaRouche PAC organizers at the Perkins Coie law firm in Seattle, Washington.

EIRNS

Zepp-LaRouche: One option which already has been publicly discussed in various publications, is the idea of appointing a new special investigator, this time to investigate Mueller, the FBI, and the role of the British—because that's what's most important. If you look at what came out in the recent ten days or so about this whole affair, there are all the signs now that the Clinton campaign, the DNC, and the Obama White House all paid the law firm Perkins Coie, which in turn paid Fusion GPS, which in turn paid former MI6 agent Christopher Steele, to produce trash. So they paid cash for trash. Steele produced this unspeakable "dodgy dossier" about Trump, which has no substance to it, but was used by the FBI and by the Clinton campaign, and by Obama, of course, to smear Trump.

Now, is that legal, to use the intelligence service— and the intelligence services of a foreign country at that—to attack your political opponent in a Presidential race? That's the real question here, and even the *Wall Street Journal*, of all places, and also the *New York Post*, and also a British newspaper called *The Week*, have all started to say that there must be an investigation of the role of the British. And if you remember, already early this year, I wrote an article saying "It's not the Russians, it's the British." That's exactly the issue: the role of the British meddling in the internal affairs of the United States, and the collusion of the secret services of the Obama administration in doing that. I think that that is the real issue.

I think that Trump should pick this up and boldly move ahead with it, because it is precisely this apparatus that brought the world so close to World War III in the confrontation with Russia just before the election.

That is one important flank. Another, maybe equally or even more important flank, is to boldly move in the direction of what the whole Russia-gate operation was aimed to prevent: Namely, to improve the relationship with Russia and with China, and do it in this upcoming Asia trip, where the potential also exists that Trump will meet not only with Xi Jinping—that is certain—but also possibly with President Putin [at the APEC summit in Vietnam], and consolidate the relationship between the United States, China, and Russia, and in that way, outflank the people trying to prevent exactly that.

Schlanger: The indications we have are that the attempt to stop this trip will not work, that the President is committed to it, and that he's made several statements about looking forward to meeting with the Chinese President.

Yet another flank that you have mentioned in the past which is very much associated with the LaRouche movement is Glass-Steagall, as a starting point toward the basic Four Laws, as a way of defeating these bankers. In the last couple of days, there has been speculation about who's going to become the new Federal Reserve Chairman, and whether [European Central Bank President] Draghi will start shedding the junk assets and so on; but so far, there's been very little talk about Glass-Steagall. This is obviously something that has to be brought forward, especially if we're going to succeed in integrating with the New Silk Road.

Zepp-LaRouche: Yes. The unfortunate, and unfortunately also not surprising news, is that the EU Commission has now implemented guidelines which prohibit the separation of the [commercial from investment] banks in the EU. That's really stupid. Because by doing that they turn away from the only way to prevent the oncoming financial crash. But obviously that's not the end of it, because in the Italian parliament, for example, there is big motion for Glass-Steagall; I know that there is even some collaboration between some people in the U.S. Congress and the Italian members of parliament on that. But I think there must be a renewed effort, because if we continue with the present system, it is just a question of time until this whole thing detonates.

And as I mentioned earlier, one consequence of the looming economic collapse is the rapid dissolution of the EU. The situation in Spain remains quite dangerous. The Spanish government of Prime Mininster Mariano Rajoy Brey outlawed the Catalan government; Carles Puigdemont, the former president of Catalonia, is now in Brussels. This could lead to a very tricky situation, because if he goes back to Spain, he could be arrested; if this crisis continues, then the Spanish government may demand from Belgium the expulsion of Puigdemont. This is European politics, you know! Obviously, there is no solution within this geometry, because the reason this conflict between the Catalans and the Spanish government exists, has everything to do with the ongoing problems of the financial system—and if there is a crash, everything could really end up in total chaos.

So, as I mentioned earlier, there is a huge effort to destroy the nation-state. I'm quite amazed that the woman from the European Council on Foreign Relations, Ulricke Guérot—this council is very much associated with George Soros—has been given quite some media presence on the First Channel of German television. She was on Deutschlandfunk this morning, pushing very hard for a reform of the EU which would get rid of the nation-state to have a Europe of the regions. This is an old policy: It comes from the Coudenhove-Kalergi, Pan-European Union—European federalists —and it's pushed by all the British media. It's the idea that you can have a Europe of only regions—maybe 50 or 60 independent regions—and then a supranational government in Brussels. Naturally, these regions, individually, would be much too weak to protect the common good of their inhabitants, while the nation-state, especially in times of crisis, is potentially the only institution which *can* defend the common good of the people.

Those who are pushing the liberal model want to get rid of the nation-state for that reason. There are some banking houses in the United States, which already years ago said the existing European national constitutions must be gotten rid of, because these constitutions

EU Commission President Jean-Claude Juncker delivers the State of the Union Address, September 2017.

were all written in the post-war period, where too much emphasis was given to sovereignty and the common good—and we should change that.

So I think this is a very important battle, and unfortunately, there is a lot of disunity in Europe. The East European countries are basically all going in the direction of working with the New Silk Road, which is much more advantageous for them; there is a new Balkan Silk Road, and there are tremendous developments in the 16+1 countries—that is, the Central and East European countries, working with China. But the only way to elevate that would be for the European governments more clearly to accept collaboration with the BRI.

But the EU has dug in its heels, and [EU Commission President] Jean-Claude Juncker, in his so-called state of the union address in September, said that the EU will now implement mechanisms to control Chinese investments. They're just stuck in geopolitics.

I have much more hope in the short term for things which could come out of this trip by Trump. If there is a positive result, then I think things in Europe will change also, because the idea that this disunited Europe could remain in opposition to Russia, China, and the

United States working together, is rather ridiculous.

So I think it is overall very dangerous. I'm not telling people to let down their guard, because the world is not yet in safe waters. But I think it's very hopeful. I appeal, again, to all our listeners and viewers to come on board the Schiller Institute. We are a very important think tank, and we have a cultural movement, fighting for a new cultural Renaissance, the idea that the cultures must be known, that people must know the beauty of the other cultures, and that all the mistrust and chauvinism, and indifference or whatever, will go away, and people will understand that the world is actually very beautiful. When Xi Jinping said, at the 19th National Congress, that China wants to work to make the whole world beautiful for all people by the year 2050, I think this is something absolutely achievable: We should all join in this effort. The Silk Road Spirit catches on, once you come to know it.

GrueneNRW

Members of the Green Party in Germany, protesting against the use of coal.

Schlanger: Helga, I have one final question for you on the situation in Europe, in particular in Germany, where you're probably the most authoritative person on these kinds of questions: What's happening with the possibility of Chancellor Angela Merkel pulling together a new government? There was just this crazy thing from the Greens, where they said they want to completely eliminate coal power in Germany by 2020. How is that going to work, with the coalition of the CDU and the CSU? Is there any way we can see a new government in Germany?

Zepp-LaRouche: It looks very difficult, because the liberal party, [the Free Democrats] already said that they will not go along with it, and it's not workable. These Greens just have a different agenda—they want to turn Germany into a Morgenthau Plan country, which says something about the authorship of their ideas.

I don't think it will work. They only agreed on the so-called Black Zero, which is the idea of debt brake, which is already in the German Constitution, unfortunately—but I don't think they have a vision. None of these parties have expressed any opinion of the New Silk Road; they have not commented on it. In part, their publications, or publications associated with them, have even opposed it. Some people are now saying it may take until next year before any results can be known; others are talking about early elections.

I think the prospects to form such a government are not exactly good; they're not exciting, for sure. My policy has always been to outflank Germany, because Germany under present conditions is too much under the control of the EU bureaucracy. But all around Germany, countries are joining the Belt and Road Initiative. I already mentioned the East and Central European countries and the Balkans. Italy is in a much more positive direction, as well as Spain, Portugal, Switzerland, and Austria. Many German cities are now waking up and creating partnerships with Chinese cities, and industrial associations are organizing local events. So, I think the idea is spreading, and the more quickly we can help it spread, the more quickly the world will get to be a better place.

Schlanger: Well, as you've emphasized, this is an unstoppable momentum. No matter what its opponents try to do, they can't stop it. But we've got to make sure it can succeed in the West. One of the most important things that we're presenting to you, the viewer, is that the Schiller Institute, as a membership organization, has been at the lead of this, going back its founding in 1984. So, check out our website. we'll be back next week, and I'm sure there'll be quite a bit more to talk about. We'll be in the middle of President Trump's trip to Asia.

So we'll see you next week, Helga.

Zepp-LaRouche: OK, bye-bye.

America's Contribution to President Xi's Vision of a 'Beautiful and Harmonious Shared Future'

by Diane Sare

Nov. 6—When he was in Federal Prison from 1989 to 1994, Lyndon LaRouche produced some of his most important and valuable philosophical writings, including a challenging introduction he wrote for the autobiography of the late Civil Rights Movement heroine and former Schiller Institute Board Member Amelia Boynton Robinson, entitled, "In the Garden of Gethsemane."

Those of us who find ourselves in Gethsemane—a Gethsemane where we are told that we must take a role of leadership with our eye on Christ on the Cross—often experience something which, unfortunately, most people do not. We tend to look at things from a different standpoint.

What I suggest often, in trying to explain this to a person who has not experienced it, is to say: "Imagine a time 50 years after you're dead. Imagine in that moment, 50 years ahead, that you can become conscious and look back at the entirety of your mortal life, from its beginning to its ending. And, rather than seeing that mortal life as a succession of experiences, you see it as a unity. Imagine facing the question respecting that mortal life, asking, Was that life necessary in the total scheme of the universe and the existence of mankind, was it necessary that I be born in order to lead that life, the sum total of that number of years between birth and death? Did I do something, or did my living represent something, which was positively beneficial to present generations, and implicitly to future generations after me? If so, then I should have

EIRNS/Nancy Spannaus

Lyndon LaRouche in prison, March 18, 1991.

walked through that life with joy, knowing that every moment was precious to all mankind, because what I was doing by living was something that was needed by all mankind, something beneficial to all mankind."

That is the beginning, I think, of true wisdom; that is the beginning of the Passion, which sometimes enables each of us when called, to walk through our own peculiar kind of Gethsemane. It is from this standpoint, that the mind of an individual such as our own, can efficiently comprehend history in the large.

The question of Gethsemane was understood in a profound way by America's founders, and expressed perhaps the most poetically by Abraham Lincoln in his

President Abraham Lincoln's second inaugural address in 1865, at the almost completed Capitol building.

Second Inaugural Address, which takes up the question of Gethsemane very precisely and specifically.

Given the extraordinary quality of Lincoln's leadership, it is not surprising that this understanding of the immortality of man would be echoed in the top ranks of his military, in this case in particular, that of the Bowdoin College Professor of Theology and Linguistics, General Joshua Lawrence Chamberlain. Chamberlain's writings about his experience in the Civil War allow us to see how it was possible that after such a bloody and impassioned conflict, which took the lives of 600,000 men, the United States could be more united and prosperous than ever before.

One of the first battles that Chamberlain fought in after enlisting was at Fredericksburg, Virginia. This battle was fought in December 1862, and might be thought of as a precursor of the ill-fated Gettysburg "Pickett's Charge," except that this time it was the Union Army charging uphill, totally exposed, toward the Rebel soldiers who were behind a stone wall in a bitterly

General Joshua L. Chamberlain

cold rainstorm. Needless to say, row upon row of men were mowed down, and after five lines were decimated, Chamberlain was part of the "reserve" as he put it, "to go in when all is havoc and confusion, through storm and slaughter, to cover the broken and depleted ranks of comrades and take the battle from their hands." ("Night on the Field of Fredericksburg," Gen. J.L. Chamberlain). This battle raged in the wet and cold for 36 hours, until the dead bodies were piled up for breastworks from behind which the living could shelter themselves. Finally at midnight on the second night, the orders came to withdraw, but the soldiers would not leave until they had buried the dead, as best they could, quietly in the dark by faint and distant starlight. Of this moment Chamberlain writes, "but heaven ordained a more sublime illumination. As we bore them in dark and sad procession, their own loved North took up the escort and, lifting all her glorious lights, led the triumphal march over the bridge that spans the worlds—an aurora borealis of marvelous majesty! Fiery lances and banners of blood and flame, columns of pearly light, garlands and wreaths of gold, all pointing upward and beckoning on. Who would not pass on as they did, dead for their country's life, and lighted to burial by the meteor splendors of their native sky?"

What could Chamberlain have been thinking of? Was he just a hopeless romantic? No, although in this mini-Dark Age we have been experiencing in the United States of late, many people would consider him so. Chamberlain, like Alexander Hamilton, generations earlier, and President Abraham Lincoln, and Lyndon and Helga LaRouche today, clearly had in mind a future world, which had not yet existed, not based on any past experience; it was a future vision, based on the necessity of the nature of man, as created in the image of God.

At any rate, the battle at Fredericksburg was not a major one in the long war, which was to rage on for three more bloody years, but it gives a sense of the intensity of the combat, and the difficulties faced by all who were engaged in the battle, on both sides.

After General Meade's failure to pursue Lee at Gettysburg, where the war might have been ended with simultaneous victories at both Vicksburg and Gettysburg, Lincoln's forecast that the war would cost many more lives, was born out during the bloody "Wilderness" campaign. It should be mentioned here that there were important international factors and implications, such as the British support for the

General Robert E. Lee, surrendering to General Ulysses S. Grant at Appomattox, April 9, 1865.

Confederacy, and the Russian support for President Lincoln's Union, which must be considered when studying the war as a whole—but the point here is to get at an important principle, which Americans must be reminded of in order to play the required crucial and positive role in the unfolding New Paradigm now before us.

Appomattox

Finally, both armies met at Appomattox, and General Lee gave the unconditional surrender that General Grant had been demanding. At that point, President Lincoln's commitment, that the nation must be pulled together "with malice toward none, with charity for all," had to be put into effect. The first thing that became clear was that in both camps, supplies were scarce, but the Rebels were actually starving, and the thin remnants of their rations had been captured by Union soldiers the day before. When General Longstreet came to General Chamberlain to tell him that his soldiers had no food, the decision was made to split the rations equally for both armies (J.L. Chamberlain, *The Passing of the Armies*, p.186). General Grant conveyed through General Griffin that Chamberlain's division, with Gen. Chamberlain at the head, was to receive the surrender, and that the ceremony should be as simple as possible, that "nothing should be done to humiliate the manhood of the Southern soldiers" (p.187). Grant had already

given orders that horses which were the property of individual Southern soldiers could be kept by them to work their ravaged farms, and that transportation should be made available to get people back to their homes as easily as possible. General Grant refused the Confederate request that they should not have to present and surrender their arms before the Union Army, however (they wanted to lay them down in a pile to be picked up later), as this was the United States to which they must now bear allegiance. Other than those few instructions, it fell upon Chamberlain to organize the surrender and design the ceremony.

Of this Chamberlain writes (p.195):

The momentous meaning of this occasion impressed me deeply. I resolved to mark it by some token of recognition, which could be no other than a salute of arms. Well aware of the responsibility assumed, and of the criticisms that would follow, as the sequel proved, nothing of that kind could move me in the least. The act could be defended, if needful, by the suggestion that such a salute was not to the cause for which the flag of the Confederacy stood, but to its going down before the flag of the Union. My main reason, however, was one for which I sought no authority nor asked forgiveness. Before us in proud humiliation stood the embodiment of manhood: men whom neither toils and sufferings, nor the fact of death, nor disaster, nor hopelessness could bend from their resolve; standing before us now, thin, worn and famished, but erect, and with eyes looking level into ours, waking memories that bound us together as no other bond;— was not such a manhood to be welcomed back into a Union so tested and assured?

Chamberlain did generate much controversy by his decision, but he reports the following observation upon conversing with several Confederate generals after the official surrender. "Their bearing was of course, serious, their spirits sad. Levying war against the United States was serious business. But one certain impression was received from them all; the were ready to accept for themselves and the Confederacy any fate our Government should dictate. Lincoln's magnanimity, as Grant's thoughtfulness, had already impressed them much."

Given the importance of President Lincoln's vision for the future of the nation, and his ever-present anguish over the suffering of the American people, imagine how the news was received by soldiers, as they embarked on the long and arduous weeks-long march home, that this beloved President had been shot at the theater on Good Friday, and died the next day—less than a week after the surrender.

After this, the role of the American military, particularly that of General and later President Grant became absolutely critical. The fact that President Lincoln had already launched the construction of the first transcontinental railroad in the middle of the war, was an important factor in uniting the nation. There were also a series of musical "Jubilees" organized by former Union Army musician P.S. Gilmore, including the first "Peace Jubilee" held in Boston, Massachusetts which featured a chorus of 10,000 voices from all over the country, and was addressed by newly inaugurated President Grant. Several of the leading opera singers involved in training and preparing the chorus were also involved in the grand opening of the Khedive Opera House in Cairo, Egypt, timed for the completion of the Suez Canal, another major project which involved officers of both the Union and former Confederate Army.

Later, in 1876, a chorus of a thousand voices would

Peace Jubilee in Boston, 1869.

sing Handel's famous "Hallelujah Chorus" at the Philadelphia Centennial Exhibition, where the United States demonstrated the revolutionary results of Alexander Hamilton's economic genius, as perpetuated by the assassinated President Lincoln's collaborators.

This exhibition had a profound effect on world affairs, and nations in Europe and elsewhere sought to emulate the American success. However, more assassinations were to follow, both in the United States and in Europe, as well as the sacking of Bismarck in 1890, which set the stage for what has been a century and a quarter of war.

The American genius Lyndon LaRouche, born in 1922, has dedicated his life to bringing the vision of Nicholas of Cusa, Alexander Hamilton, and Abraham Lincoln, into reality. President Xi Jinping has echoed the same intent with his speech before the 19th Congress of the Communist Party of China, with his commitment to the "happiness" of the people and a shared future which is both "harmonious and beautiful." The current visit of President Trump to China opens the potential that a U.S.-China relationship could shift the world in that direction. Its success will depend upon the willingness of the American people to remember our universal identity as LaRouche and Lincoln have understood it.

April 1, 1998

The Principles of Long-Range Forecasting

by Lyndon H. LaRouche, Jr.

During recent years, I have repeatedly defined a "New Bretton Woods" reform of international financial and monetary institutions. In a presentation to a March 18, 1998 seminar, held in Washington, D.C., I summarized that package of proposals once again, situating the package in the setting of the current series of global, financial, and monetary crises.[1] In this present report, the presentation of the hitherto almost unknown principles of long-range forecasting, is preceded by situating that topic, and its importance, within the relevant features of the presently ongoing, systemic breakdown of the world's financial and monetary institutions.

During the 1992-1994 interval, the downward-bent, currently ongoing economic process, which has been engendered by nearly thirty years of increasingly bad policy-shaping, had entered its terminal boundary layer.[2] Since this 1992-1994 phase-shift in that process,

the plunge toward the already impending death of the present system, has been neither reversed, nor moderated, but, rather, significantly worsened, by every effort of governments and international financial authorities, to deny, or to avert the onrushing, general financial catastrophe.

The 'Triple Curve,' Again

The author's familiar triple curve (**Figure 1**) identifies that 1966-1997 process which has led into the planet-wide, systemic financial and monetary crisis of October 1997-January 1998. The relevant features of that Figure are summarily described as follows.

A reversal of the direction of post-World War II policy-shaping, which began during 1964-1968, underlay the British sterling crisis of Autumn 1967, and the immediately ensuing U.S. dollar crises of the first quarter of 1968. In the U.S. case, policies motivated by "post-industrial utopian" ideologies, were initially introduced into actual U.S. government economic practice during 1966-1967, with an immediate, resulting decrease in the net rate of physical-economic growth in the U.S.A. By 1970-1971, the net growth of the U.S. economy, as measured in physical-economic terms, reached a net-zero balance, between increase of output and acceleration of attritional effects. With the introduction of the

---

1. A transcript of the March 18 address is published as Lyndon H. La-Rouche, Jr., "Toward A New Bretton Woods," *Executive Intelligence Review*, March 27, 1998. A "ninety-minute" video edition of the actual March 18 address has been published.

2. See, the author's 1992 Democratic Presidential campaign address on the subject of "The Great Mudslide," broadcast under the title, "The Man George Bush Fears the Most," on the ABC-TV network, on Feb. 1, 1992. (Reported in Brian Lantz, "LaRouche on TV: Voters Listened to the Wrong People!," *Executive Intelligence Review*, Feb. 14, 1992.) The quality of "boundary layer," is typified by its characteristic, geometrically increasing turbulence, producing periodic shocks, all leading into a region of discontinuity. There are significant similarities to what Bernard Riemann defines as the entry of a continuously accelerated projectile, within a tube of indefinite length, into the transsonic region [Bernhard Riemann, *Über die Fortpflanzung ebener Luftwellen von endlicher Schwingungsweite*, "On The Propagation of Plane Air Waves of Finite Magnitude," *Bernhard Riemanns gesammelte mathematische Werke*, H. Weber, ed. (New York: Dover Publications reprint, 1953)]. At

that latter point, efforts to continue the system beyond that discontinuity, result in either an hyperinflationary, or hyperdeflationary chain-reaction mode of disintegration of the entire system. The 1921-1923, hyperinflationary efforts of Germany to meet the Versailles conditionalities, are an example of such a boundary layer. The present impact of both IMF and "Maastricht" conditionalities, is of the same species of folly as the 1921-1923 Germany hyperinflation.

FIGURE 1

A Typical Collapse Function

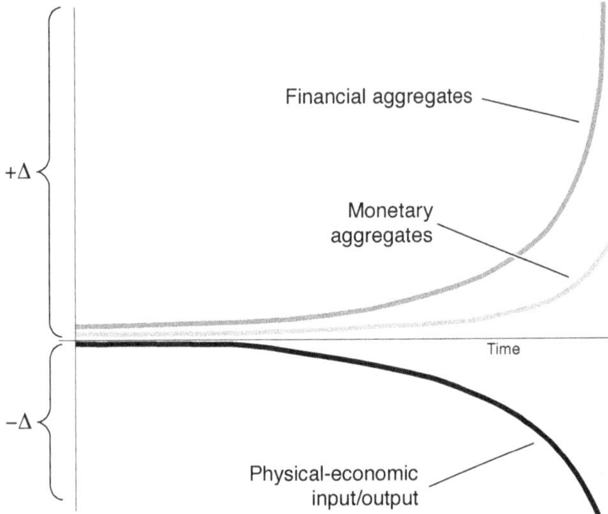

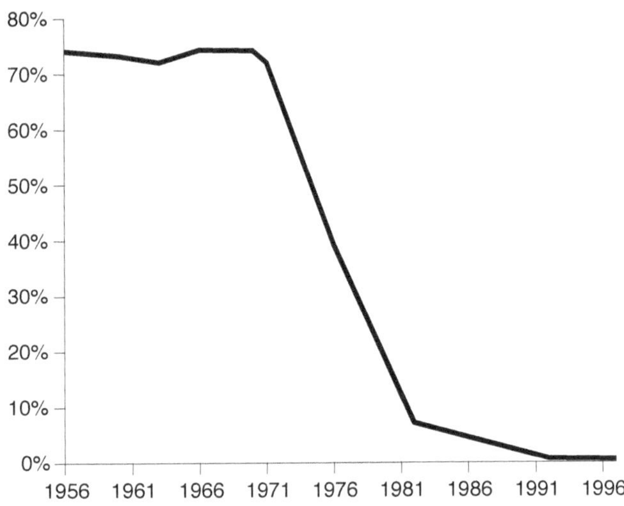

FIGURE 2

U.S. Import-export Trade as Percentile of Foreign Exchange Turnover

"floating-exchange-rate" monetary system, in 1971-1972, the U.S. economy, *as measured in physical-economic terms,*[3] has enjoyed a rate of annual contraction of more than 2% each year, to the present date.

Coinciding with that zero-balance which the U.S. economy reached in 1970-1971, the world's financial and monetary system underwent a fundamental phase-change in its functional characteristics. This change is reflected most simply in the decline of the percentile of total foreign-exchange turnover attributable to combined imports and exports. In the U.S., for example (**Figure 2**), in the 1970s through 1990s to date, this disastrous change, to a "floating-exchange-rate monetary system," was reflected in the new trend, world-wide, toward moving financial investment out of infrastructure, production, and trade, into pure financial and monetary speculation. In the new, post-August 1971, global regime, the greatest portion of financial investment moved into domains ever more remote from the real economy: Petrodollars, junk bonds, and derivatives.

Taking the 1966-1971 and 1972-1997 intervals as one, we have the "Triple Curve" presented in **Figure 1**. Beginning 1966, expansion of both monetary growth (e.g., M3) and financial aggregates, moves upward, in terms of physical-economic measurements, relative to

a decline in total investment (infrastructure, capital, labor, etc.) in real production and physical distribution of goods.[4] It becomes increasingly clear, from 1967-1968 onwards, that continued net nominal (financial) growth, is obtained chiefly through expanding monetary aggregate, at the expense of looting of the total historical investment in the productive sectors. The increase of financial aggregates becomes increasingly dependent on nominal (fictitious) financial capital gains, the which, in turn, reflect, not production, but the increasingly complex relations between compounded appreciations which are based on nominal price-earnings ratios, and increase of monetary aggregates. Thus, the changes in curvature among the three depicted curves, are not statistical, but functional in nature. The

____

3. E.g., Lyndon H. LaRouche, Jr., *So, You Wish to Learn All About Economics?* 2nd ed. (Washington, D.C.: Executive Intelligence Review, 1996).

____

4. I.e., as measured in physical-economic terms. See LaRouche, op. cit. The Triple Curve is constructed as follows. First, the combined (household, production, infrastructure) market-basket, per capita of total available labor-force, of combined physical, education, science, and health costs, of present and prior intervals, are compared in physical, not monetary terms. The relative upward, or downward direction of per-capita changes in net physical output, is measured, first, in physical market-basket terms, not money-prices. The result of that comparison is plotted (i.e., the lowest among the three curves in the figure). In order to compare current physical output with monetary developments, the physical output is equated to current money prices of the per-capita market-basket constituents. Thus, the relationship between the lowest of the three curves and the scale of monetary turnover (e.g., M3) is measured. Finally, the price of the current volume of total financial aggregates outstanding is added: the top-most of the three curves. See also, footnote 9.

function thus portrayed, is the "medical" chart showing that the patient is a dying, self-doomed system.

The combination of "bail-out" and increasingly savage, anti-human, austerity measures, imposed by governments and financial institutions, has had the net effect of being financially inflationary, in the sense of the similar 1921-1923 developments in Weimar Germany (**Figure 3**). The result of these putatively stop-gap efforts, has been to increase, rather than moderate, the intensity of the forces which underlie, and determine the outbreaks of successive storms of crisis on the surface. These measures have wasted large masses of the pre-existing, real capital assets, which were better expended in the economic-recovery efforts of a new system, to replace the presently doomed one.

Typical are the net results of what were presumed to be those stop-gap measures adopted during the 1995 Halifax monetary conference. Those measures were intended to delay the plunge into what was, in fact, the then-already looming, financial-derivatives-driven end-phase of the system. The intent was to delay what was in fact the inevitable, to a time beyond the relevant 1996 elections.[5] These measures postponed the onset of the next round of crisis on the surface; but, they also made the later crises, striking us during late 1997 and 1998, more rapid, and far more severe than would have been the case, had the necessary radical changes not been postponed, by the misguided decisions of the Halifax conference.

There is a relevant, most urgent political lesson to be learned from such heretofore typical, recent decades' failures of leadership among the G-7 and other governments. That failure of the Halifax meeting, while typi-

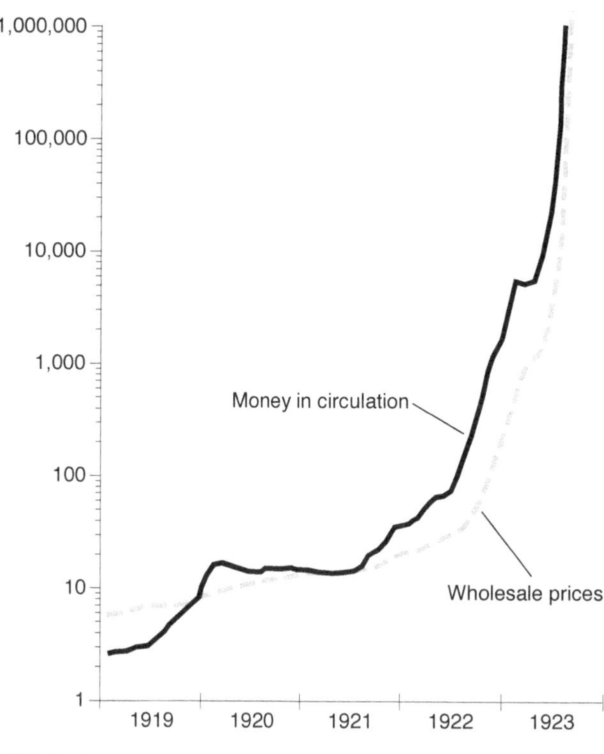

Source: Knut Borchardt, "Wachstum und Wechsellagen 1914-1970," in Hermann Aubin and Wolfgang Zorn (eds.), *Handbuch der deutschen Wirtschafts- und Sozialgeschichte*, Stuttgart: Klett, 1976, vol. 2, p. 699.

cal of the intellectual mediocrity pervasive among the recent crop of heads of government and leading political parties, must also remind historians of the folly of Germany's "young Moltke," who, in 1914, fled from the risk of obtaining an early and pre-assured military victory, by dissipating the concentration of resources essential to victory, into a fool's errand, dispersing that concentration to levels below the critical level needed for the right-flank assault, for the silly purpose of seeking to minimize, needlessly, a wide assortment of relatively irrelevant varieties of risks.[6] Such behavior in the political command of today's nations, should remind us, fondly, of "Organizer of Victory" Lazare Carnot's successful replacement of such defective kinds of general officers by, in some notable instances, selected,

---

5. From the period of the Halifax conference, see William Jones, "Clinton Puts Financial Reform on International Agenda," *Executive Intelligence Review*, June 23, 1995. Jones wrote that the "reform" mechanisms specified in the Halifax communiqué "are useless to manage the global financial disintegration now under way—an impossible task." Among recent discussions of the Halifax decisions, see U.S. Treasury Secretary Robert Rubin's press briefing of Feb. 19, 1998, where he discussed a "new financial architecture": "Even as we address today's financial instability in Asia, the G-7 will also focus on efforts to reform the international financial architecture to better prevent crises in the future and to better manage them when they occur. We in the United States have been focussed on this for quite some time. As you may remember, the President took the leadership with respect to what became known as the Halifax initiatives. And more recently, over quite some number of months now, the Federal Reserve Board and Treasury have been working together on this question of architecture." The issue is discussed in Michael Liebig, "Biggest Bailout in History Still Won't Save World Economy," *Executive Intelligence Review*, Jan. 23, 1998.

6. On "young Moltke's" folly, see Andreas Ranke, "Schlieffen, Carnot, and the Theory of the Flank," *Executive Intelligence Review*, Feb. 6, 1998.

more effective sergeants.[7]

The performance by the consensus among leaders at Halifax, would be described most charitably, by comparing it to a group of unemployed actors engaged in theatrical try-outs, competing for the role of Shakespeare's self-doomed Hamlet. Such is the shilly-shallying pragmatism of fearful political leaders, controlled by their desperate attempts to deny the fact, that the present world economy, like that of the U.S.A. and western Europe, in particular, has already collapsed far below the quality of thirty years ago, with doom not far ahead.

In fairness to the individual leaders who participated in that wretched consensus, in their capacity as individual personalities: that pathetic behavior of the group as a whole, reflects the qualities of performance sought in the selection of today's leaders. That defective mode of performance, is what selected leaders are strongly advised to adopt. See the image of Rembrandt's "Belshazzar's Feast"—such behavior of societies and their leaders, is characteristic of the self-doomed, presently existing political system of today's nations, and of the institutions of today's "global community." Such folly as exhibited at Halifax, is not the result of any randomly determined coincidence of bad leadership by particular officials. The folly represents nothing less than what is demanded of today's national leaders by the self-doomed, present political system at large. In any case, such cowardly zeal to deny the fearful evidence, is today's potentially fatal, tragic flaw, the leading source of danger to global civilization.[8]

My definitions of the "Triple Curve" function, show the relevant internal dynamics of the present financial-monetary system: From this boundary layer, now, and already then, in 1995, the present global financial and monetary system, as it has evolved since 1967-1971, could never emerge alive from the passing of this century.[9]

With the onset of the forecasted, October 1997 outbreak, of a new phase of this systemic crisis of the international financial system as a whole, global financial conditions had become wildly turbulent. This evidence of qualitatively increased density, and global scope of turbulence, should be recognized as a reflection of the financial process's extreme nearness to the outer limits for continued existence of the entire, global system.[10]

---

7. In 1792, Carnot was elected to the Legislative Assembly; after the Reign of Terror began in 1793, he was named to the Committee of Public Safety. He took all military operations under his control, for France's war against Austria, Prussia, and Britain. In 1793-1794, he formed a new, mass-based army; organized the military forces for total war; and concentrated his military efforts on attacking the English. See Dino de Paoli, "Lazare Carnot's Grand Strategy for Political Victory," *Executive Intelligence Review*, Sept. 20, 1996.

8. This type of denial is not an accidental, but, rather, a characteristic pathology of the "Baby Boomer" generation's heritage of university campus-based, mid-1960s youth counterculture. This pathology, concentrated within the influential university-student strata of the generations born after August 1939, has produced a radical form of cultural relativism, typified by the "Rainbow Coalition" phenomena, known as "politically correct" language and related codes of behavior. The essential characteristic of this cultural relativism, has infected the "New Age" strata within two succeeding generations. Notably, today's "political correctness" is copied, intact, from Nazi Propaganda Minister Josef Goebbels' *Gleichschaltung*, and also from the Communist parties of the U.S.A., and elsewhere, during the 1920s through 1960s. Spawned within such "Orwellian" regimes, this perversion now marches under the banner of the U.S. National Endowment for Democracy and kindred trade-styles. It is also characteristic of the code of "political correctness" specific to the neo-conservative yahoos of Speaker Newt Gingrich's following, and to the kindred neo-fascist currents, within the labor movement and elsewhere, of the present-day Lovestoneite tradition of the Communist International's so-called Right Opposition. Another, related, leading source of this type of "political correctness" in speech and related codes, has been the so-called "Frankfurt School," established for the explicitly adopted purpose of carrying out nihilist and Freudian-Marxist Georg Lukacs' corrosive program for destroying western European civilization from within. The essential characteristic of all varieties of political correctness, the programmatic outlook of the Rainbow Coalition included, is compulsively exegetical modes of sophistry, or, in short, lying with a fraudulent explanation. By this ruse, a calamitous, thirty-year decline in the U.S. real standard of living, is called progress; the exegetical fraud behind this outright lie (that the economy is fundamentally sound), is the sophistry, that, since the downward changes in real standard of living are correlatives of progress toward the paradise of "post-industrial society," we must judge today's conditions by "post-industrial," not real-life standards of performance. Such pathological behavior, in the service of "political correctness," should be recognized as an outgrowth of that dogma of cultural relativism, which denies the existence of those universal truths, upon which the U.S. Declaration of Independence and Federal Constitution were absolutely premised.

9. This schematic was introduced in the author's address to a conference of the International Caucus of Labor Committees and Schiller Institute in Eltville, Germany, on Dec. 2, 1995, and was published, on page 4, in *Executive Intelligence Review*, Jan. 1, 1996. See also the Presidential-candidate's address on Martin Luther King Day, published in *Executive Intelligence Review*, Feb. 2, 1996. For a more recent discussion of the elements of the figure and their interaction, see the author's speech to the ICLC-Schiller Institute conference in Arlington, Virginia, on Jan. 17, published in *Executive Intelligence Review*, Jan. 30, 1998.

10. Lyndon H. LaRouche, Jr., "What Economics Must Measure," *Executive Intelligence Review*, Nov. 28, 1997.

Beyond the 'Ides of March'

At the time my referenced March 18, 1998 Washington, D.C. address was delivered, the inevitable Ides of March had just been reached. The international system had just experienced the first burps of yet a new round of crises for the second quarter of 1998, a crisis far more turbulent, more intense, with wider, chain-reaction impact, globally, than that which had erupted during late October 1997.

It is more than merely conceivable, that this new round of turbulence could detonate that chain-reaction collapse of the derivatives bubble, which would not only disintegrate virtually every central banking system of the planet, but produce that effect within as brief an interval as several panic-stricken days. A more cautious estimate would be, that this will be the penultimate shock, prior to the next round, when refusal to adopt the author's policies, would make virtually certain, that the world's economic system would plunge, like Mozart's guilty Don Giovanni, into the impatiently waiting abyss.

Acknowledge this to be the situation. Then, suppose, that the majority of today's shapers of economic policy, otherwise recognized as the political establishments' "free trade" and "globalization" fanatics, aided by the "young Moltkes" of 1998, were to succeed in preventing the early adoption of the kind of "New Bretton Woods" agenda which this writer has specified. In that case, the presently erupting, new, April-June resurgence of this crisis, will accelerate the present, terminal phase of the world's systemic, financial and monetary turbulence, thus bringing the world to, if not over the edge of a waiting abyss. That abyss is the imminent threat of a collapse of civilization into a "New Dark Age," similar to the Fourteenth Century "New Dark Age," but, this time, on a planetary scale.

Thus, during the second quarter of 1998, the world is, once again, experiencing an attempt, led by wild-eyed monetarists of the Mont Pelerin Society type, to meet yet another round of global financial-monetary crisis. Their Pavlovian response to each crisis, continues to be a combination of sundry hyperinflationary financial-monetary measures, with predatory extremes of austerity, and other tactics for "bailing-out" private financial institutions. A likely, new repetition of such habituated, morbid lunacy, if it were not prevented, would appear in the form of a maddened horde of political flagellants' stubborn repetition of the disastrously failed tactics, employed in response to the earlier, year-end "Asia crisis." The fabled, failed, doomed King Canute could not have been more pathetically tragic.

For a brief time, if only in the opinion of very gullible persons, such wildly desperate, blind-ideology-driven measures, like the doomed, hyperinflationary stock-exchange bubbles of February-March 1998, might succeed, like the eye of a hurricane, in moderating the surface turbulence of the present, April-June round of the crisis. Then, during that brief interval of relative calm, the world's great fools would agree to say, as they had done repeatedly earlier: "Let us pretend that the storm has passed. Let us pretend, that our system as a whole is 'basically sound.'"

In reality, contrary to such childishly hysterical huddling of leaders in their mental fox-holes, this time, their actions themselves would push the global system to, or even over the edge of a virtually "thermonuclear" form of debacle, either as a Weimar Germany-type of hyperinflationary disintegration of the system, or reversed financial-leverage implosion of the world's $140 trillions-plus financial bubble. Without the measures of reform I have proposed, the implosion of that bubble would plunge the world into a Fourteenth-Century-style "New Dark Age," this time on a planetary scale.

To repeat the crucial point presented in the March 18 address: If the world is to avoid such an impending, general collapse into a "New Dark Age," a leading group of sovereign nation-states, which might be otherwise known as "We, the Survivors," must act to initiate a sudden, and radical turn, even over the objections of any number among other nations: to adopt arrangements, best compared for similarities with the Bretton Woods rules of the 1950s period of post-war economic reconstruction. Without the virtually immediate adoption of those changes, in rules of monetary exchange, international finance, and trade, which I have therefore identified as the needed, "New Bretton Woods" measures, it is assured that the world would be plunged, very soon, into a planetary "New Dark Age."

As emphasized in that address: The sudden and radical, proposed measures of financial and monetary reform, are indispensable, but not sufficient by themselves.

The world requires a design for a new, stable, global financial and monetary order. The purpose of this, is to create the pre-conditions under which an immediate trend of physical-economic recovery is possible. Without such radical changes in the financial and monetary system, no physical recovery of the world's economy could be expected earlier than the middle of the Twenty-First Century.

That mid-Twenty-First-Century recovery, if it were to occur, would be preceded by an intervening period of, perhaps, two generations, a terrible period of deep demographic collapse through factors of famine and disease. The monstrous developments in Russia, since the end of 1991, including a stunningly precipitous demographic collapse, are a foretaste of the horrible fate which will grip all nations of this planet, should the indicated "New Bretton Woods" not be installed during the weeks and months immediately ahead. The rapid collapse of our planet's population, to the levels of no more than several hundred millions, is a plausible scenario under such conditions.[11]

To prevent this catastrophe, the indicated changes in financial and monetary rules are indispensable.

Although those specifications for new financial and monetary rules are indispensable, I do not suggest that such necessary changes, by themselves, will cure our problem. Like the great reconstruction of the 1946-1966 period, under old Bretton Woods rules, a good financial and monetary system itself, could not create a recovery spontaneously. Such a system does little more than create the pre-conditions under which it is possible to launch a sustainable form of economic recovery. The Bretton Woods conditions of the 1950s, did not cause the post-war economic recovery in Europe. The Bretton Woods rules of Harry Dexter White, et al., helped by the marginally crucial role played by the modest flow of Marshall Plan funds, contributed the conditions without which the economic-recovery programs of sovereign governments could not have succeeded as they did.[12]

So, the new rules, which my associates and I have presented for immediate adoption, are designed specifically to create the preconditions favorable for what is fairly described as a global, Franklin Roosevelt-style economic recovery.[13] The object of the design, is the fostering of large-scale, productive capital formation, permitting the successful use of new sources of credit, mobilized for this purpose by sovereign governments.

The world requires accelerating rates of new, real

---

11. The case to study, for comparison, is what is termed Europe's collapse into a "New Dark Age" of the mid-Fourteenth Century. This was the result of approximately a hundred years of devolution of European civilization, following the death of the Holy Roman Empire's Frederick II, a degeneration of Europe, under Guelph League hegemony, which culminated in the inevitable collapse of the Europe-wide Lombard banking system of the mid-Fourteenth Century. During this period, approximately half the pre-existing parishes of Europe were wiped from the political map; during the terminal phase of this century-long moral, political, and economic degeneration of Europe, the population collapsed by no less than one-third. The repetition of such a terminal collapse of the present world financial and monetary system, would quickly reduce the "carrying capacity" of this planet, from over five billions, at present levels of practiced technology, to no better than a world population of several hundred millions, and that within a period of not more than approximately two generations. The world is not threatened by an "Armageddon," but, rather, something between the import of "Belshazzar's Feast" and the doom of Biblical Sodom and Gomorrah: the end of a culture which had willfully abandoned its moral fitness to survive.

12. Predominantly, the reform adopted at the war-time conference, held in Bretton Woods, New Hampshire's Mount Washington Hotel, was the product of the influence, reflected in President Franklin Roosevelt, of a group of U.S. historians and economists reflecting the tradition of Benjamin Franklin, Alexander Hamilton, Mathew Carey, Friedrich List, and Henry C. Carey. (See *Political Economy* feature, in **Executive Intelligence Review**, March 20, 1998.) While President Roosevelt lived, the new, post-war, international monetary system was intended to function as an integral part of Roosevelt's patriotic determination to eliminate all colonialism, and also the dominant influence of British economic liberalism, at the close of the war. With the death of Roosevelt, and the role of Stimson and others in inducing Harry Truman to order the effectively worse-than-useless nuclear bombing of Hiroshima and Nagasaki, the British and their co-thinkers were able to prevent Roosevelt's post-war "American Century" reforms, from being carried through as intended. The role of Harry Dexter White, as contrasted with the contrary influences of John Maynard Keynes, should be noted; these differences dominated the often contradictory tendencies within the post-Roosevelt functioning, 1946-1971, of that monetary system. Although Germany received a much smaller ration of Marshall Plan aid, per capita, than Britain or France, Germany's performance was vastly superior to either of those neighbors. The reason for Germany's superior financial performance over its neighbors, is centered in the U.S. government's acceptance of banker Hermann Abs' proposal for establishing a Franklin-Roosevelt-style institution, Germany's *Kreditanstalt für Wiederaufbau*. Additionally, however, it should be noted that the superiority of Germany's economy, over those of Britain and France, since 1876-77, is Germany's use of its world-leadership in science, then, as a driver for its copy of that 1861-1876 model of the American System of machine-tool-design-driven agro-industrial progress which had been launched, under U.S. President Abraham Lincoln, by the world's then leading economist, Henry C. Carey. As a result of the combination of this American model and the measures associated with the *Kreditanstalt für Wiederaufbau*, Germany did not tolerate the kind of waste of its Marshall Plan funds, which caused the inferior performance of Britain and France.

13. The emphasis here, is Roosevelt's intended post-war measures: to end, immediately, all colonial systems; to terminate the domination of the world market by the British "Eighteenth-Century methods" of "liberal economics;" and, to make available to the liberated former colonies, as to the nations of Central and South America, the opportunity to participate in the economic methods and technologies of progress enjoyed by the United States itself. In short, what we supporters of the Non-Aligned Nations' effort, were pleased to identify as a "just new world economic order."

capital formation in agriculture and industry, with emphasis upon high rates of technological progress. However, such economic renewal would not be possible without the inclusion of a massive infrastructure-building program, planet-wide. Without that latter program, global economic recovery of per-capita physical output would not be sustainable, and, in many regions of the world, could not even begin. Nor would such an infrastructure-building program be possible, without the proposed "New Bretton Woods" financial and monetary reform, reversing supranational authorities' hitherto persisting nullification of those preconditions for freedom and democracy, which can be sustained only under the rule of technologically progressive, perfectly sovereign nation-state republics.

The world must be transformed immediately into a system of partnership among sovereign nation-states, as American System advocate Friedrich List laid the foundations for the modern European national economy, or, as President Charles de Gaulle envisaged such partnership among the perfectly sovereign nation-states, "from the Atlantic to the Urals."[14] Without that change, the needed high rates of physical-capital formation, could not be achieved and sustained. Without the proposed monetary reforms, re-establishing the sovereignty of nation-state republics, a viable economic recovery could not be organized.

The Lesson of Versailles

So, in its leading features, the presently needed "New Bretton Woods" must be viewed as a set of rules designed not to provide, but to foster a kind of general economic reconstruction. This is an economic reconstruction similar to that which lifted Europe and other parts of the world out of the ruinous conditions imposed upon national economies by the Versailles Treaty, and by the ensuing depression and World War II.

It should be stressed that the processes, including the rise of Adolf Hitler in Germany, leading into World War II, would not have been possible without the persistence of a global environment created by those same "Economic Consequences of the Peace" which were the principal, forecasted results of Versailles.[15] We must look back to the lessons to be learned from studying both of the conditions which the Versailles system generated: the systemic crisis of 1920s Germany, and the cyclical depression of the 1930s. With the effects of that depression, and its ensuing war, in view, we must focus upon the initial period of reconstruction in progress throughout the 1946-1957 interval. We must apply those successful precedents, not as patented, or otherwise perfect models;[16] the crises of the 1920s and 1930s were predominantly expressions of a global cyclical crisis, whereas the present crisis is a global systemic one.[17] With that crucial distinction in mind, we must study the 1946-1957 period of post-war reconstruction, as a source of insight into some of the similar, if more challenging, features of the present case.

Then, at the close of World War II, the task of financial and monetary reform, was undoing the evils of Versailles. The "new Versailles," today, is those prevailing

---

14. The "Europe from the Atlantic to the Urals," envisaged by President de Gaulle, has no congruence with the return to the political institutions of Europe's Middle Ages and the 1618-1848 "Thirty Years War:" the Maastricht agreements imposed upon continental Europe by such foaming-at-the-mouth, rabid German-haters as Britain's Prime Minister Margaret Thatcher and de Gaulle-hating French Socialist President François Mitterrand. These were the same pair which launched the post-1991 Balkans War, which like the Entente Cordiale's launching of the pre-World War I Balkan Wars, had the purpose of drawing Russia, Austria, and Germany into a war of mutual destruction, by aid of which Britain, assisted by its French poodles, might exert virtual supremacy over continental Europe.

15. John Maynard Keynes, *The Economic Consequences of the Peace* (New York: Harcourt, Brace and Howe, 1920). The circumstances for Adolf Hitler's Autumn 1923 rise from obscurity, and later, London and Harriman family-backed rise to power, in 1933, were, like the moral degeneracy of 1918-1943 France, made possible by the conditions imposed upon Europe by Versailles. However, that does not mean that Versailles made Hitler's rise to power inevitable. What made Hitler, and World War II "inevitable," was the repeatedly successful intervention of, chiefly, London and New York bankers, to crush all those forces, like the German patriot, Dr. Wilhelm Lautenbach, whose anti-Versailles programs of economic reconstruction, could have made Hitler's London-backed rise to power impossible. Just so today; if the cabal of powerful lunatics, centered around London's financier oligarchy and Robert Bartley's *Wall Street Journal*, succeeds in defeating those who work to overturn the present globalist system, then the worst result is inevitable. Who were then to blame for the result? The incurably evil financier-oligarchs and their lackeys—or the cowardly, corrupted ordinary citizen, who declines to support those, upon whom the future life of the citizens' children, grand-children, and great-grandchildren may depend absolutely?

16. E.g., the folly of the Eisenhower Administration, from 1954 on, in following the advice of Arthur Burns, thus setting into motion the financial bubble expressed as that deep, 1957-1960 recession, which erupted in February 1957.

17. On the distinction between the past cyclical (e.g., "business cycle") crises, and the present, planet-wide, systemic crisis, see Lyndon H. LaRouche, Jr., "What Economics Must Measure," op. cit., and, also, the concluding section, subtitled "The Business Cycle," of Lyndon H. LaRouche, Jr., "Russia Is Eurasia's Keystone Economy," *Executive Intelligence Review*, March 27, 1998, pp. 51-52.

policy-shaping trends of the recent thirty-odd years, which have now plunged us into this presently ongoing, global, systemic, economic-breakdown crisis. The Bretton Woods rules of the 1950s, provide us many applicable precedents for those radical reforms essential for lifting the world's economy out of the different quality of systemic nightmare, created by that "new Versailles," the which is the recent thirty years' trends in policy-shaping.[18]

The 'New Bretton Woods'

To this effect: compare the results of two monetary systems: a) the old Bretton Woods agreements, up to the point of the U.S. manned landing on the Moon; and, b) the results of changes in policy-shaping, hegemonic since 1971-1972. Compare these systems in terms of directions and rates of change in physical-economic output, as measured per-capita and per-square-kilometer of relevant surface-area of our planet (**Figure 4**). There is no doubt that, by comparison of performance, the outcome of the post-1972 period of a "floating-exchange-rate" system, has been worse than a great error; it is a disaster. As we have stressed, once again, here, there are significant qualities of difference between the conditions of the 1950s and today; nonetheless, there are but a few important differences of detail, between the old Bretton Woods, and the form in which its useful moral and juridical precedents should be revived now.[19]

Otherwise, the principles of successful reconstruction itself remain, if only broadly, the same as those which led into the fabled "economic miracle" achieved under Germany's Chancellor Konrad Adenauer.

All these considerations, when combined, require a radical change, not only in financial and monetary policies, but also a profound change, away from the recent decades' thinking about economics, the which latter has become hegemonic among virtually all among the world's governments and financial institutions.

To that end, it is the included purpose of the present report, to show, that had the latter institutions employed a competent notion of long-range economic forecasting, at any time during those changes of the recent thirty-odd years which have ruined us, rational governments would not have tolerated those policies, which have now brought this world to its present brink of a planetary "New Dark Age" abyss. We would not have tolerated the kind of thinking which became hegemonic during the recent thirty-odd years.

From the vantage-point defined within this report, there is no mysterious cause for the world's present dismay. The bad policies which have ruined the world's economy, were choices made under the influence of that generally accepted, but increasingly defective, so-called "mainstream" opinion, which has dominated, increasingly, the selective shaping of policies of govern-

---

18. The 1950s of Italy's Alcide de Gaspari, Germany's Konrad Adenauer, and, at the close, Charles de Gaulle, represents the "take-off" period of European post-war reconstruction. These were the years of relatively tight exchange controls, and related protectionist measures by sovereign nation-states, restrictions which were essential to establishing the foundations for the achievements of the pre-1971 1960s. Thus, the way in which the Bretton Woods system functioned during the 1950s period of relatively tight, dirigistic forms of financial and monetary restrictions, is the phase of the old Bretton Woods system most usefully referenced in addressing the increasing disorderly, tumultuous present circumstances and their inevitable near-term aftermath.

19. The principal difference required, is the replacement of the past role of central banking systems, by "Hamiltonian" national banking. Given the ratio of current obligations to current GDP, virtually all of the world's central banking systems are already hopelessly bankrupt. While we can ensure the continued functioning of all the socially necessary private banks through government-supervised bankruptcy-reorganization, the central banking systems themselves are no longer capable of generating adequate supplies of credit. They could not even maintain the present levels of employment, production, and trade. New credit must be generated by the power of sovereign governments, a measure balanced by writing off in excess of $140 trillions equivalent, globally, of derivatives and other largely fictitious financial assets, and by rewriting much short-term and medium-term legitimate debt, as long-term debt at yields in the order of 1% to 2% annually.

The Failure of Post-1971 Economic Policymaking

The charts in **Figure 4** show three series, for comparison.

In Series 1 (Figures 4.1.1-4.1.0) you see the cancerous growth-rate of financial turnover in the United States, in the period 1971-1973 to the present. Indicative sub-categories of turnover are shown, of money flows into mergers and acquisitions, money flows into futures speculation on interest rates, on currencies and equity indices, and so forth. Overall in the United States, valuations of stocks, debts, and especially, since the mid-1980s, derivatives, have grown at hyperbolic rates. Worldwide speculation in derivatives shows the same cancerous growth rate.

Series 2 (Figures 4.2.1-4.2.0) shows the decline

U.S. Merchandise Trade as Percent of Global Dollar Currency Trading

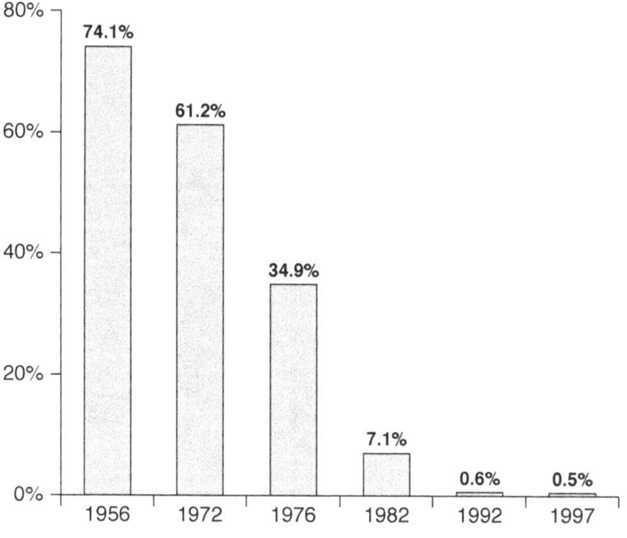

Annual U.S. Financial Turnover

(trillions $)

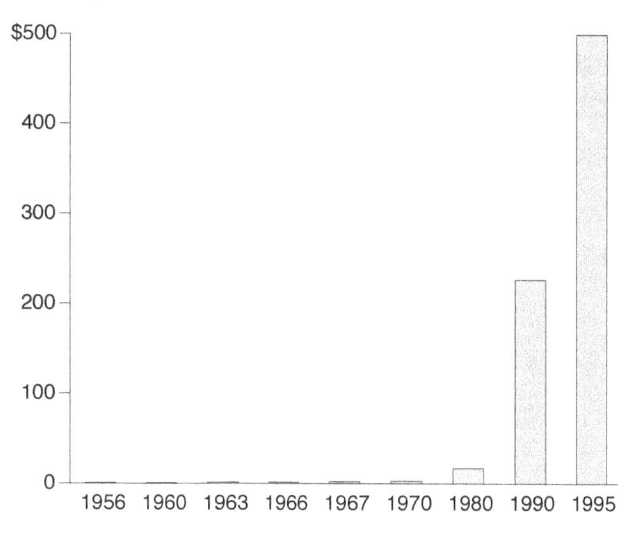

ment and relevant private institutions, during most of the recent thirty-odd years. Had rational governments foreseen the outcome of such "mainstream opinion," they would have acted to resist such opinion, and also uproot it by aid of the most vigorous re-education of an economics-illiterate, duped general public.

For related reasons, without the added adoption of that needed standard of long-range forecasting now, as a guide to, and integral feature of future policy-shaping, the possibility of successfully managing the needed recovery would be jeopardized.

Never again, must we allow governments to do as the failed, neo-liberal architects of the floating ex-

in money flows into investments into basic production sectors of all kinds in the U.S. economy, over the same time period that, in contrast, financial speculative turnover ballooned. Also shown, is the related decline in proportion of the U.S. workforce engaged in essential activity in these sectors. The percentage of workers (as a share of all operatives), and the percentage of investment (as a percent of the Gross Domestic Product) have declined over the period from 1971-1973 to the present, for manufacturing, agriculture, basic physical infrastructure (water, power, transportation, etc.), construction, and related categories of activity. This does not reflect increased productivity; just the opposite. The declining productive investment and employment show up as declining rates of production and consumption levels per household in recent decades. The final graph of this series, illustrates one aspect of this devolution of the economy, in terms of the deteriorating condition of an average household. In the 1960s, the pay-check of the principal wage-

earner, would cover the four basics shown (home, car, food, health care), with money remaining for other essentials; at the same time, households were productively engaged in the economy. Today, households can no longer exist on the pay-check of the principal wage-earner—typified by the recourse of family members to hold, among them, several jobs per household. At the same time, the numbers of jobs in non-productive activities in the economy have proliferated—typified by casino employment, part-time fast-food jobs, and all kinds of non-essential services.

In Series 3 (Figures 4.3.1-4.3.0), you see the deteriorating composition of U.S. national product, in terms of even such a crude measure as Gross Domestic Product. It is obvious how the value is dropping in the period 1971-1973 to the present, of the component of GDP related to manufacturing and goods production, relative to the rise in value of financial, insurance, real estate, and related non-productive services.

—Marcia Merry Baker

Hyperbolic Growth of the U.S. Financial Aggregate

(trillions $)

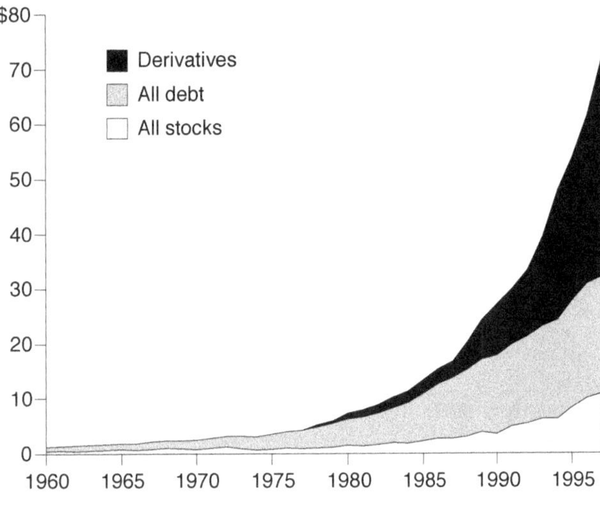

Financials Dominate Futures Markets

(millions of contracts traded)

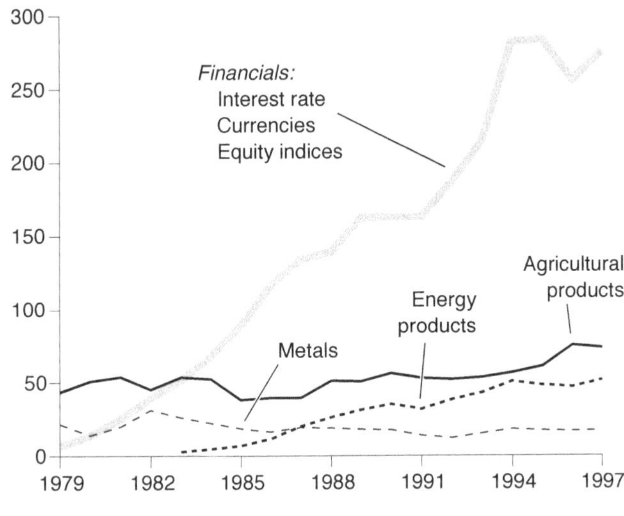

change-rate system did. Never again, must we allow the kind of ranting, romantic ideologue's compelling emotional impulses, mere prejudices, to override discretion in choosing a route of travel in economic development. Never again, must we permit ranting ideologues, like the flagellant hordes of the Fourteenth Century, or today's wild-eyed Heritage Foundation fanatics, to menace the public welfare, or permit our economies to be directed by deranged ideologues, to an H.G. Wells', or related style of proposed sociological utopia.

Instead of demanding "politically correct" conformity with today's prevalent madness, with prevailing blind faith in popularized ideological fads and their virtual-reality agendas, check the actual route of travel implied, beforehand. Hereafter, nations must check carefully, in advance, the character of terrain through which the proposed route of travel actually leads.

This brings us directly to the core subject-matter of this report.

Up to this time, no government of the recent quarter-century, or other relevant leading institution of the same period, has yet become sufficiently competent to define adequately the policies needed, in the aftermath of the adoption of a New Bretton Woods monetary order. Although the appropriate methods of long-range forecasting remained chiefly in obscurity, even among otherwise competent economists of an earlier, happier

period, even those qualified competencies have chiefly vanished from leading "mainstream" policy-shaping opinion today. Three decades of impact of a declining culture, globally,[20] have produced the state of affairs, in which, with few exceptions, even among the relatively best relevant professionals, most lack competence, in the specific degree the present circumstances of crisis require competence.

In these matters, a relative few among professionals contribute useful suggestions; worse, so far, even those professionals are not likely to discover adequately ap-

---

20. Franklin Roosevelt had the advantage of counsel provided by a patriotic tradition among historians and economists. This "American System" tradition of Franklin, Hamilton, the Careys, John Quincy Adams, Henry Clay, Friedrich List, and Abraham Lincoln, persisted, even after the unfortunate U.S. Presidencies of Teddy Roosevelt, Ku Klux Klanner Woodrow Wilson, and Calvin Coolidge, as a strong, if minority current in U.S. academic and related life, until the unfortunate developments, which followed the historically most untimely death of Franklin Roosevelt. It was systematically purged from the textbooks and the universities, by the burgeoning influence of the neo-Jacobin rabble of epistemologically cretinous Frankfurt-Schoolers and intellectually kindred leftists and neo-conservatives, during the middle to late 1960s, and beyond. Hence, few professionals of the 'Sixty-Eighter generation of university graduates, have any competence at all in matters of political-economy and actual history. President Clinton, who suffers conspicuous short-comings of this sort, is otherwise a relatively superior intellect, among the representatives of his own and the succeeding generations of professionals. On more general implications of the cultural decline of European civilization during the Twentieth Century: that as a sub-topic is better treated in the relevant location of this report, below.

Mergers and Acquisitions versus Manufacturing New Plant and Equipment

(billions $)

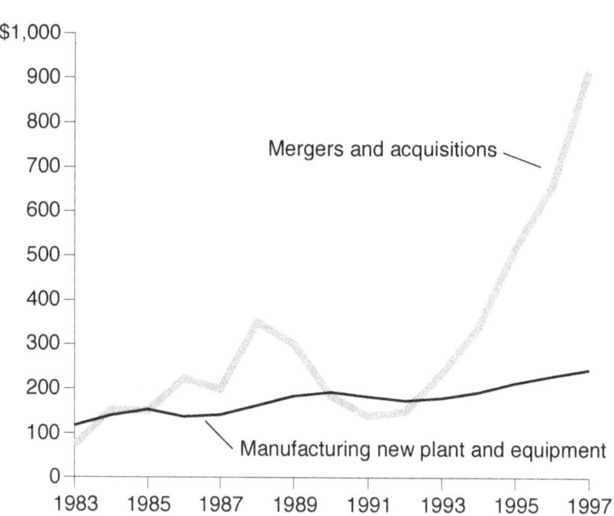

World Derivatives Growth: the Cancer Takes Over

(trillions $)

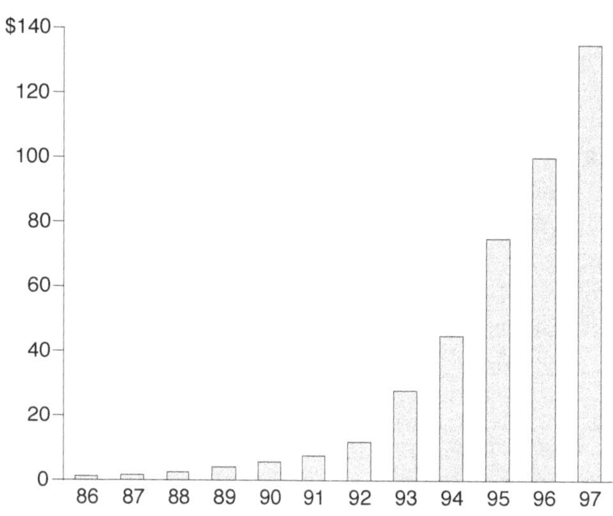

propriate answers, until they have, first, corrected their habitual thinking, in the degree wanted for identifying the relevant questions. Earlier, I have identified and summarized the essential features of that matter, of long-range forecasting. We continue that discussion here, extending it to its bearing on both the design and management of a physical-economic recovery program.[21]

The Task of Forecasting Defined

In any rational use of that term in today's economics practice, "long-range forecasting" signifies the selection of choices of any present day's policies, according to the foreseeable consequence of one's choice not less than seven or more years ahead, usually one to two generations ahead. Usually, as in respect to the 1964-1972 roots of the presently worsening global economic disaster, it has been changes in axiomatic features of cultural outlook, from one generation to the next, which are of the relatively greatest significance, in directing the effects of policy-shaping along either an upward, or a downward track in effects.[22]

Within the relatively narrow framework of the relative best among those doctrines of recent decades' industrial and agricultural practice, the which are to be found under the rubric "economics," three interacting factors of cost, determine the minimum duration ("horizon") such forecasts must span. These three are: 1) Capital-intensity, and correlated energy-density, of investments in infrastructure, agriculture, and industry; 2) Simple physical depletion, through wear-and-tear, of capital improvements; 3) Relevant rates of technological attrition. The following, unavoidable costs of profitability, are thus derived: 1) What are the rates at which maintenance of existing capital stocks must be pro-

---

21. See the discussion of this matter, under the sub-heading of "Marx's blunder on technology," in Lyndon H. LaRouche, Jr., "Russia Is Eurasia's Keystone Economy," *Executive Intelligence Review*, March 27, 1998, pp. 47-51 (see footnote 17). Since this involves conceptions and principles unknown to most professional economists, and relevant others, it is necessary to include here a restatement of the argument made earlier, in those pages.

22. In general, it is during childhood and adolescence, that the axiomatic assumptions of the coming new adult generation are instilled. Most crucial, is the portion of each generation which is destined to dominate, through promotion, the policy-shaping strata of leading private and governmental institutions, a generation to a generation-and-a-half later. It is not necessarily the case, for all time, that the capacity for original, axiomatic discoveries should tend to evaporate beginning about twenty-five years of age [Cf. Lawrence S. Kubie, "The Fostering of Scientific Creativity," *Daedalus*, Spring 1962]; nor, need the exceptions be limited to the relatively tiny, and still shrinking number of true thinkers among today's matured professionals. However, whatever the brighter prospect for the future, the tendency for creative sterility among matured professionals has been the dominant trait of modern populations until this point.

vided?; 2) What are the minimally required rates of replacement?; and, 3) What is the required, combined rate of technological progress and energy-density, per-capita of labor-force? Otherwise, in general, what, in broader terms, do these specified requirements also imply?

To lay the basis for the answer to those questions, I must proceed now, first, by repeating, in summary, several points which have been characteristic of my work in, and teaching of economics[23] during the recent forty-five years, since the outcome of a study conducted during the 1948-1952 interval.[24] During all of that time, from 1951-1952 to the present, my treatments of economics and long-range economic forecasting, have

---

23. This included the teaching of a one-term introductory course on the subject of Marxist economics, at several campuses, during each term of the 1966-1973 interval. The burden of that course, was to point out the needed principal correction in Karl Marx's four-volume **Capital**: the blunders derived from his admitted, if sometimes ambiguous exclusion of "the technological composition of capitals," and those respecting the notions of "value," and of what constitutes "productive" labor, in various, mutually contradictory locations within those volumes. This was the same difference I enjoyed, on the subject of economics, in my sundry dealings with professedly Marxist organizations and academics during the 1950-1973 interval. Marx's blunder was rooted in two axiomatic features of his adult life's work. First, as in both his pre-1848 attacks on Friedrich List, and his later attacks upon Henry C. Carey, both of which he conducted at the insistence of Frederick Engels, Marx was obsessively addicted to the neo-Frondist defense of the landed aristocracy of Dr. François Quesnay, and, in defense of the financier oligarchy, to both the Venetian ideologue J. Sismondi, and to the "only scientific" secretions of such lackeys of the drug-pushing British East India Company, as Adam Smith and David Ricardo. Second, Marx was most strongly addicted to a variety of "materialism," which combines the tradition of the ancient Greek reductionists, and Paolo Sarpi's neo-Ockhamite empiricism. On both accounts, Marx was incapable of recognizing the determining role of individual cognition in economic and other social processes.

24. As reported in sundry published locations, this study, elaborated during the 1948-1952 interval, was initially prompted by reaction against the plainly fraudulent aspects of Professor Norbert Wiener's attempt to impose his radically positivist, mechanistic "information theory," upon the content of human communications. At the beginning of the 1950s, the present writer had recognized the "ivory tower" follies of John von Neumann's "systems analysis," as genetically (axiomatically) the same thing as Wiener's bungling. The initial standpoint of the present writer was his earlier work in defense of Gottfried Leibniz's monadology, against the attacks on Leibniz central to Immanuel Kant's **Critique of Pure Reason**. In fact, as the present writer discovered later, Kant's argument was based upon Leonhard Euler's folly of *petitio principii*, in his own mechanistic attack upon Leibniz on the issue of the **Monadology**. The same axiomatic fallacy, in its guise as "linearization in the very small," is the most common of the crucial incompetencies inhering in all widely accepted doctrines of political economy today, those of Adam Smith, David Ricardo, Karl Marx, and von Neumann, et al., included.

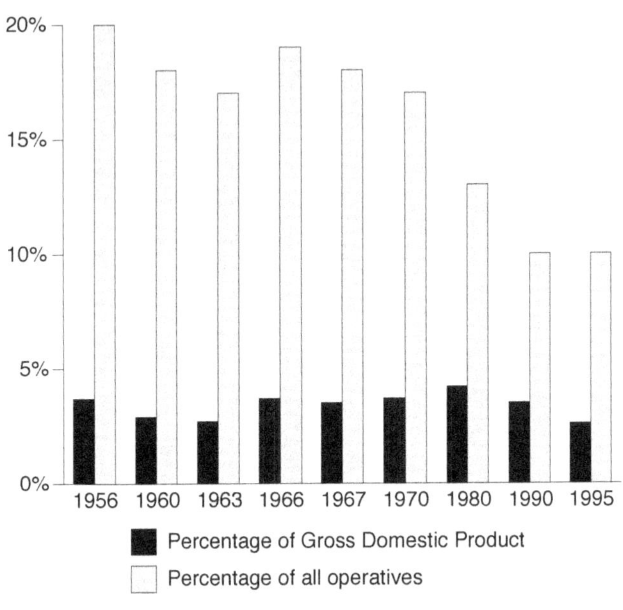

Manufacturing Investment and Employment

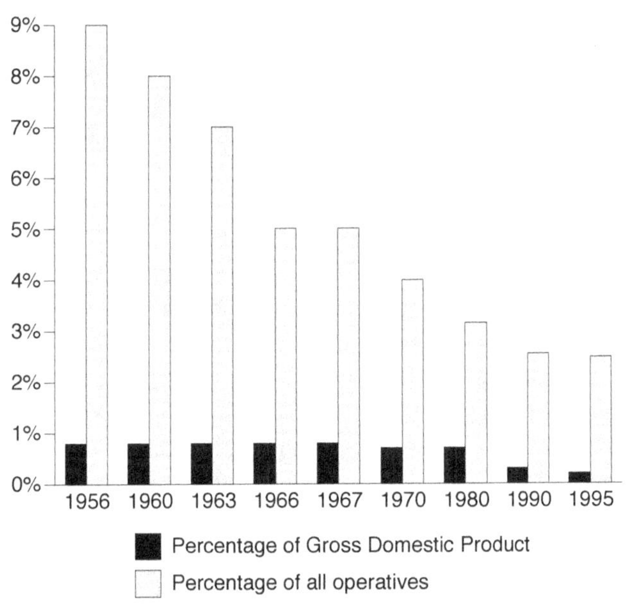

Agriculture Investment and Employment

been consistently premised upon the following axiomatic specifications:

1. The sole source of increase of the human species' potential relative population-density, per capita and

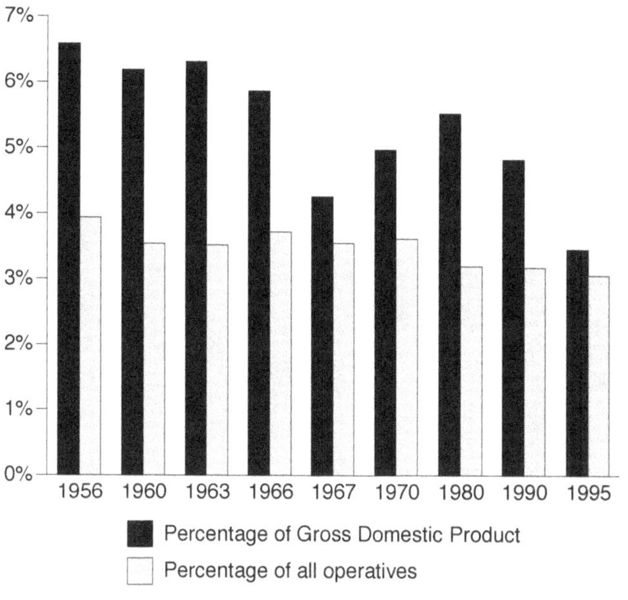

FIGURE 4.2.3

Construction Investment and Employment

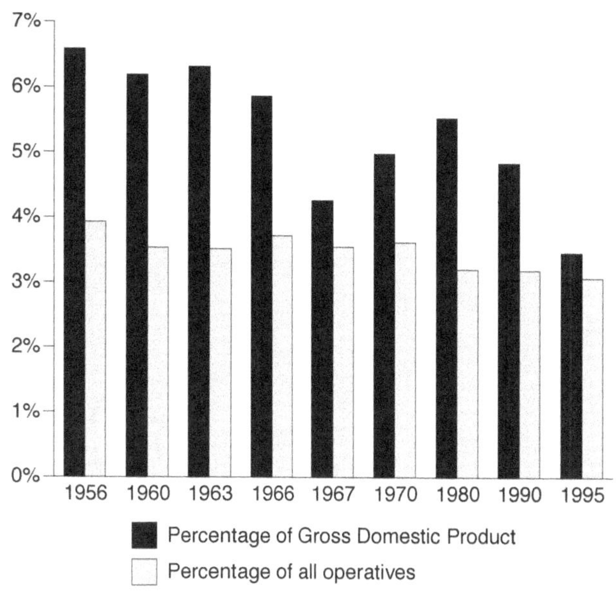

FIGURE 4.2.4

Basic Physical Infrastructure Investment and Employment

per square kilometer of the Earth's surface, is "anti-entropic" changes in the physical characteristics of the outcome of human social behavior, changes which depend upon continued scientific and technological progress. Not only is such progress the sole source of increase of the productive powers of labor; without such progress, human cultures inevitably degenerate, "entropically."

2. Those discoveries of principle of artistic composition, which are prompted by the defining function of metaphor in Classical modes in poetry, tragedy, music, and plastic art-forms, have an even higher degree of significance than discoveries of physical principle. Indeed, it is only when we view physical science as a branch of Classical art-forms in general, that we may comprehend adequately both physical science as such, and also recognize the mode in which both the principles of Classical artistic composition and science combine, in an indispensable way, to affect man's social mastery of nature, and to effect the variously upward, downward, or stagnating modes in culture generally and political-economy in particular. Indeed, all proper practice of statecraft is governed implicitly by application of the principles of the greatest compositions in Classical art, to the definition of history, as history is to be viewed from this standpoint.

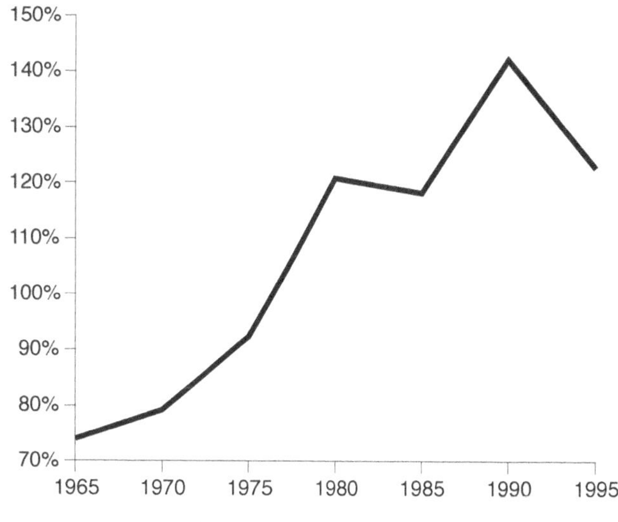

FIGURE 4.2.5

Combined Home, Car, Food, and Health Insurance Payments as Percent of Average Paycheck

Let us now presume a readership which is at least moderately literate in the view of science from the Classical standpoint, as this standpoint is typified by the distinguishing, axiomatically common features of the work of Nicholas of Cusa, Leonardo da Vinci, Johannes

Goods-production Portion of GDP as Percent of Total GDP

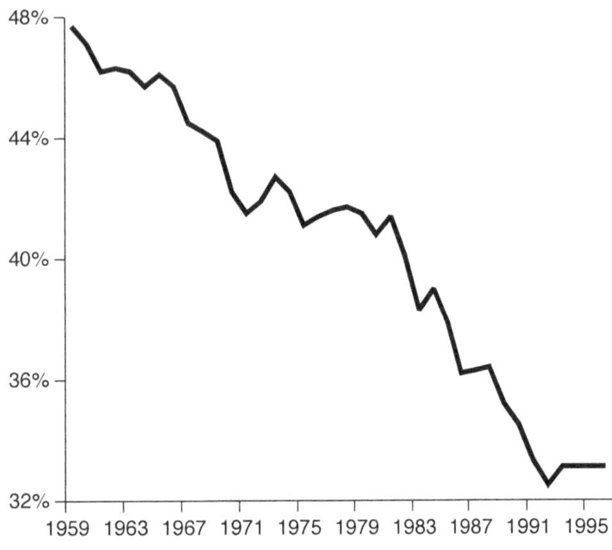

Gross Domestic Product, by Component: Goods Production versus Services

(percent of total GDP)

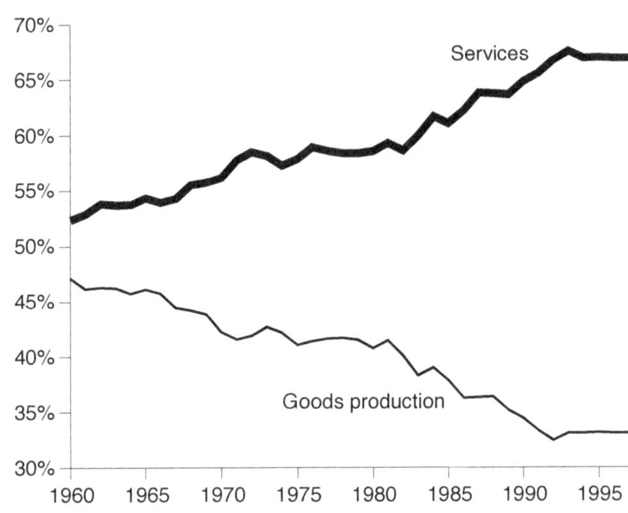

Kepler, Gottfried Leibniz, Lazare Carnot, Gaspard Monge, Carl Gauss, Bernhard Riemann, et al. It is a readership also literate, even if not immoderately so, in the metaphor-based fundamentals of composition, specific to Classical forms of poetry, tragedy, music, and perhaps also some among the Classical forms of plastic arts. This is a reader able to think of history, as essentially the history of development and practice of ideas, that from the same standpoint as the Classical approach to physical science and art.[25] For purposes of optimizing clarity for such an audience, here, a certain pedagogy is indicated.

That presumed, begin where I began, back during the 1948-1951 portion of my 1948-1952 study. From the outset, my adopted task was to show that Wiener's application of his mechanistic "information theory," both to living processes, and to human cognition, is, in both immediately implied cases, biology and cognition, absurd in fact, and wicked in its consequences for physical science, as also for general social practice.[26] The

---

25. The author uses the term "ideas," only in a sense entirely consistent with Plato's definition. *Ideas* are discoveries of either validated, universal physical principles, or validatable resolutions of Classical forms of metaphor in art and political history. The latter resolutions of metaphor have the same form as validated discoveries of universal physical principles. Notions sustained merely by sense-certainty, by deduction, or by symbolic argument, are not "ideas."

26. For reasons of the epistemological illiteracy predominant in European culture since the late-Eighteenth-Century hegemony of the axi-

omatically reductionist, Anglo-Dutch and French "Enlightenment," there has been a persisting difficulty in reckoning with the empirical fact, that living processes are determined by an entirely different ordering-principle, than the implicitly entropic destiny of all processes which appear to be representable in terms of algebraic functions (i.e., functions which assume Leonhard Euler's anti-Leibniz, fraudulent, *petitio principii* defense of the reductionist presumption that linearity prevails in the very small). From Luca Pacioli, Leonardo da Vinci, and Johannes Kepler, onward, the distinction between the types of ordering which appear as the qualitative, empirical distinctions between living and non-living processes, had been a subject of fully rational inquiry. The political triumph of reductionist lunacy, during the course of the Eighteenth Century, banned rational thinking about such distinctions. Thus, the empirical fact of distinction in ordering (e.g., *mathematical [e.g., hypergeometric] cardinality*) between living and non-living processes, became a playground for spinning irrationally mystical, obscurantist sophistries. "Vitalism," is an example of the irrationalities engendered by attempting to define this empirical distinction from the reductionist's "politically correct," algebraic standpoint. Thus, after the political hegemony of the fraudulent, reductionist notion of universal entropy, introduced, during the middle of the Nineteenth Century, by Clausius, Grassmann, Kelvin, et al., the problem of differences in ordering between living and non-living processes was broadly recognized by referring to the ordering of living processes as anti-entropic. Especially after the work of Ludwig Boltzmann, which refined the mechanistic notion of entropy in terms of gas theory, the general expression for the distinguishing characteristics of ordering, between living and non-living processes, became "negative entropy." Sorcerer Bertrand Russell's apprentices, Norbert Wiener, for "information theory," and John von Neumann, for economics and "brain theory," insisted that "negative entropy" must be derived exclusively from within the reductionist's statistical models premised axiomatically upon the Euler-Lagrange-Laplace-Cauchy, politically correct, but fraudulent presumption of linearity in the extremely small (and, also,

GDP, by Component: Manufacturing vs. Finance, Insurance, and Real Estate

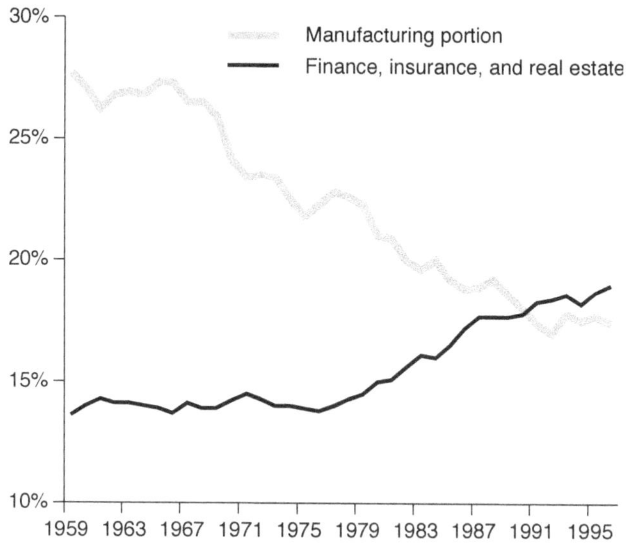

Financial Aggregate's Growth versus Growth of Goods-production GDP

(trillions $)

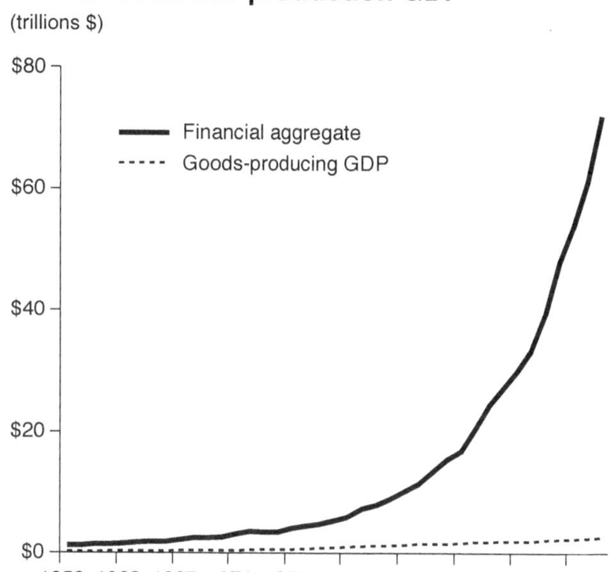

starting-point chosen for this undertaking was the subject of cognition, as we define the term "cognition" here, immediately below. The strategy for this initial phase, assorted the empirical effects of cognition between two seemingly parallel, but actually coinciding expressions of validatable, original discovery of principle: discoveries, or re-discoveries[27] of validatable new physical principles, and ideas generated as validatable resolutions of Classical metaphor. During the work on this project during the 1948-1951 interval, the two tracks were developed in parallel, and then brought

---

the extremely, astrophysically large). Thus, the contemporary radical empiricists (e.g., logical positivists such as Wiener and von Neumann) presume life to be determined within the bounds of reductionist dogma. Therefore, this is overtly, or implicitly their choice of basis for viewing life as a kind of secretion ("epiphenomenon") of processes which may be defined statistically. They extend this same fraud to phenomena which are peculiarly characteristic of certain living species: e.g., man. So, they define "brain function" (e.g., the doctrine of "artificial intelligence"), and, therefore, also "information."

27. E.g., as by students in a Classical-humanist mode of education, in which students are not permitted merely to *learn* physical and artistic principles, as from textbooks and classroom lecture-notes, but are obliged to *know* them instead. To *know* a principle means to re-enact the original discoverer's mental experience of generating that conception. In the case of the student trained in the latter mode, that person does not rely upon eidetic memory of a learned formulation and procedure; instead, that person's mind regenerates the conception, rather than calling it up from "memory banks."

together. Later, in 1952, the work of Bernhard Riemann was taken into account, as providing the needed strategy for introducing notions of measurement, into the discoveries which had been developed up to that point.

The role of physical science in physical economy, as the latter is axiomatically distinct from empiricist schools of political-economy, was the original benchmark chosen for these studies. The actual experience of the modern industrial process, was the context for the initial attack upon the issues implied. In other words, the "machine-tool principle," as implied by the work of Leibniz, and as introduced to generalized practice, during 1792-1794, by France's Lazare Carnot. The pivot of this phase of the study, was the fact soon known to any reasonably intelligent university undergraduate: that a well-designed apparatus, which provides proof-of-principle demonstrations for a newly discovered physical principle, is the pivot by means of which validated discoveries of physical principle, are translated into those new designs of products and processes, by means of which, in turn, the per-capita and per-square-kilometer productive powers of labor are advanced.

The flow-chart presented here as **Figure 5**, illustrates the nature of the connection between validated

discoveries of new physical principles, and the technological progress,
in the form of man's increased power
over nature, per capita and per
square kilometer of the Earth's surface, into which these discoveries
lead. I now summarize the immediately relevant features of my argument on this subject, as given on numerous earlier occasions.

If one attempts to describe the
effect of repeated such insertions of
new technologies, into the physical-
economic process of the society/
economy taken as an indivisible
whole process of the human species'
self-reproduction, the following
result appears immediately.

1. The potential increase of the
potential relative population-density
of a society,[28] is bounded by the
number of valid, implicit, discovered
physical principles known, and thus
available to be expressed in the form
of applicable new technologies of individual and social practice.

2. However, the realization of the
benefits of discovery and prolifera-
tion of scientific and technological
progress, is conditional upon the way
in which social relations define the
communication of validated products
of cognition, and in which social relations themselves are ordered to this
ultimate effect.

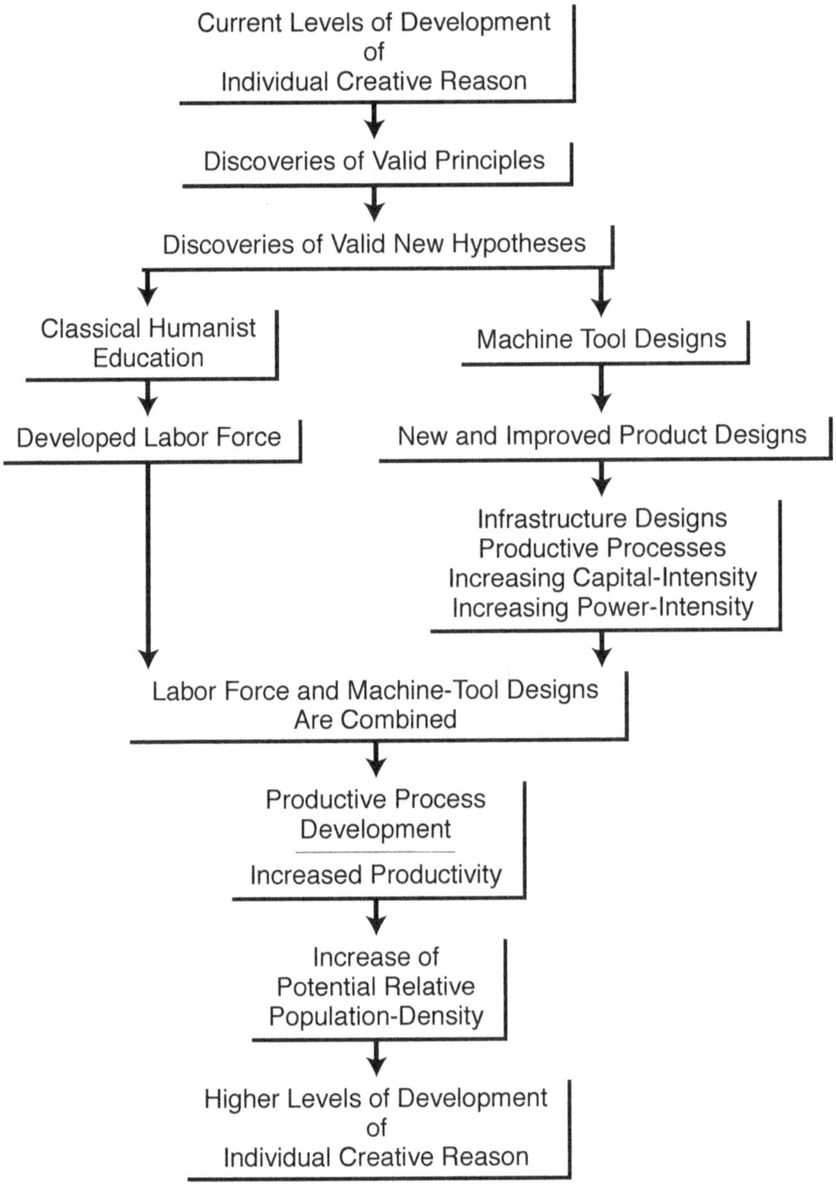

The deepest challenge to compre-

FIGURE 5

The Machine-Tool-Design Principle

---

28. This is not limited to the simple number of persons in a population which is self-sustained through technological progress. The increase in potential, per capita and per square kilometer of the Earth's surface, is conditional upon related improvements in the demographic characteris-tics internal to households, in addition to the demographic characteris-tics of population more simply defined. This multiply-connected func-tion is also conditional upon the improvements of land-area, as through development of basic economic infrastructure. The function so implied, is conditional upon maintaining the rate of growth of potential relative population-density so defined.

hension posed by these historical facts, is concern for
knowing the *ontological* nature of individual human
cognition itself. That task is a fully comprehensible
one, at least respecting all its axiomatic measures, if
one approaches the matter as I did, throughout the
1948-1952 interval. I approached this task from the
standpoint of refuting Immanuel Kant's devotion of his
life's work, especially of his last decades', to defaming

Gottfried Leibniz.[29] Leibniz's view of these matters, which I defended, and employed for the both the initial, 1948-51 study, and for its 1952 sequel, is a modern affirmation of the notion of the *idea* also specific to the Socratic dialectical method of Plato. For the purposes of our topic here, the crucial significance of this point is as follows.[30]

Usually, the original, or pedagogically replicated discovery of a validated, universal physical principle, is prompted by a perplexing paradox of the following, ontological type. For this purpose, assume the history of the internal development of European science, from Egypt, through Classical Greece,[31] through the succession of leading intellects of the Platonic Academy of Athens, and related cases, such as Archimedes, into the founding of modern experimental physical science through the influence of such writings as Nicholas of Cusa's ***De docta ignorantia***.

Given, a notion of geometry as exemplified by the practice of Plato's Academy.[32] Also, given, Cusa's emphasis upon a notion of a science susceptible of representation in terms of measurement, and in the form of a geometrically-based mathematical description of measurable results. Given, such a case, in which the previously established physical science of reference, was already premised upon experimental proof-of-principle measurements. Now, take note of the increasingly frequent case in the history of modern European science, in which nature presents an empirical case, which all then-extant, accepted science appears to have been ordained to have been impossible.[33] For pedagogical purposes, take the case in which none of the array of specific, universal physical principles previously adopted is invalidated, except in the respect that the assembly of those principles, taken as a whole, appears to exclude the possibility of the troubling empirical evidence.

If the empirical evidence supporting, respectively, the "old physics" and the reality of the contrary phenomena, are equally valid, empirically, then no deductive or statistical-mathematical solution for the contradiction exists. The conflict is thus defined as an *ontological paradox*, in the sense illustrated by Plato's

---

29. During the 1948-1951 interval, for the purposes of that project itself, the author's references to Kant's work were almost entirely focussed upon the **Critique of Pure Reason** and a few collateral writings. The writer's view was informed by his adolescent commitment to defense of Leibniz's principle of *monadology* against Kant's attack, there, on this and closely related features of Leibniz's work. (Also, Leibniz's related principle of the universality of non-constant curvature in the extremely small interval of action.) Originally, Kant had been Prussia's leading disciple of Britain's David Hume, and a rabid adversary of Leibniz from that standpoint. As Kant indicates in a report featured within his **Prolegomena**, he turned away from Hume, when Hume, later, adopted a more radically empiricist view in respect to "moral philosophy." Kant did not drop his enmity toward Leibniz at that point, but, rather, resorted to a pure-and-simple Aristotelean standpoint, rather than Hume's more radically Okhamite standpoint. The Classical attack upon Kant's later work, notably on the issues of morals and aesthetics, is that of Friedrich Schiller.

30. Here follows a recapitulation of the same argument supplied on pages 47-51 of the referenced earlier report.

31. Although Greek civilization had depended chiefly upon Egypt for the foundations of its own progress, Classical Greece added a crucial element, an element not visible in specialists' reports of their studies of ancient Egypt. The simplest indication of that distinction, is the comparison of Greek Classical sculpture (e.g., Scopas, Praxiteles) with its Archaic Egyptian and Greek predecessors. The difference between the Archaic and the Classical, is the conscious employment of the principle of the *idea*, as Plato best represents conscious use of that principle. Certainly, *ideas*, so defined, existed in all those changes which increased, directly or indirectly, all the human species' progress in increased potential relative population-density; the distinction of Classical Greek culture, is both the appearance of consciousness of the principle of the *idea* as such, and, decisively, the role of such consciousness in enabling mankind to secure conscious, willful control over the process of fostering and employing such *ideas*.

With respect to Asia, the case is less clear. There is intimation of the notion of an *idea*, in Panini's treatment of the Vedic-Sanskrit, an intimation which correlates with the long-cycle features of early Vedic (e.g., 6,000-4,000 B.C.) solar-astronomical calendars. In contrast, early Mesopotamian lunar astronomy is defective, relative to Greek, Egyptian, and Vedic-Sanskrit cultures. Recent developments in China, create the circumstances in which the study of early Chinese culture's roots, from this standpoint, should be placed on the agenda; the general impression of what might be found, is positive.

32. For this purpose, the contemporary and correspondent of Archimedes, the Platonic Academy's Eratosthenes, provides a bench-mark.

33. For model cases, two are implicitly referenced illustrations in the structure of this argument. The first is the empiricist Leonhard Euler's *petitio principii* hoax, attacking Leibniz's **Monadology**: Euler's fraudulent denial of Leibniz's demonstration of the implicit universality of non-constant curvature in the infinitesimally small. Euler's fraud was effectively overturned by the development of principles of hypergeometry, successively, by Carl Gauss and Bernhard Riemann. Note Gauss's precedence in his discovery of the orbit of the asteroid Ceres, and Riemann's 1854 habilitation dissertation, *Über die Hypothesen, welche der Geometrie zu Grunde liegen*, **Bernhard Riemanns gesammelte mathematische Werke**, H. Weber, ed. (New York: Dover Publications reprint, 1953). The second is the work of a collaborator of both Gauss and Riemann, Wilhelm Weber, in his proof-of-principle demonstration of the absurdity of J. Clerk Maxwell's politically-motivated exclusion of the Ampère "longitudinal force" from Maxwell's account of electrodynamics. On the latter see Laurence Hecht et al., "The Significance of the 1845 Gauss-Weber Correspondence," **21st Century Science & Technology**, Fall 1996. The latter case will be expanded by ongoing attention to the related implications of the work of Ampère's collaborator, Fresnel, respecting the principles of electromagnetic propagation, including so-called "gravitational waves."

Parmenides dialogue. As Plato emphasizes, in that and other locations, the failure of the Eleatic reductionist school of Parmenides (like the school of Plato's adversary, Aristotle, later) is located in the axiomatic inability of deductive-reductionist modes of thinking, their intrinsic inability to comprehend the process of change, which bridges the genetic change separating a relatively superior, from a relatively inferior species of scientific or other thought.[34] That factor of change takes us out from the bounds of deductive method; no deductive method can master such a challenge.

Nonetheless, the problem is not an insuperable one: all fundamental scientific and Classical forms of artistic progress, alike, attest to the existence of that faculty of the individual person's cognition, the which, adequately developed, can infallibly solve any ontological paradox, rooted in a validated conflict of empirical evidence. This faculty is the characteristic, implicitly "anti-entropic" principle of action, the which is expressed by a well-developed capacity of the individual's cognitive powers.

The difficulty is, that while we enjoy well-established notions of experimental proof-of-principle, by means of which we can test the validity of a proposed solution to such a paradox, there exist no possible means, by which the sense-perceptual apparatus of an observer could comprehend the mental processes, by means of which that validated principle itself was generated. Nonetheless, there are other means available to experimental physical science, through aid of which those processes can be known directly by another mind. If two minds generate a common, experimentally validated solution for such an ontological paradox, the common validation, provides one of those minds certain knowledge that the relevant mental process experienced in his, or her mind, was the same type of mental process which occurred in the other mind.

Thus, we have the picture displayed by the flow-chart presented here as **Figure 5**. In modern agro-industrial society, the most important medium for transforming validated discoveries of physical principle into man's increased power over nature, per capita and per square kilometer, is the role of the machine-tool-design principle, as outlined by this flow-chart.

Focus upon the function which education must fulfill, in order that the continuation of such progress can be predetermined. Conversely, what we have to say, on this account, here, may be rightly taken as also pointing to the moral and intellectual bankruptcy of popularized recent changes in policy of public and higher education. The view of education expressed here, while admittedly viewed as an egregious one by current "mainstream opinion," is key for comprehending how the mind works, and for understanding the principles upon which competent long-range forecasting depends, that absolutely.

Classical Humanist Education

The essential empirical distinction of the human species from all lower beasts, including, presumably, that professed great ape known as the Duke of Edinburgh,[35] is the relevant archeological and other evidence of human existence, dating from, implicitly, more than a million years ago.[36] The principal evidence

---

34. "Genetic" is employed here in the sense of the meaning Plato supplies for use of the term *hypothesis*. Use the geometry of Euclid as the background against which to define "hypothesis." In such a geometry, the ultimate test of whether an empirically plausible proposition may be adopted as a theorem of the geometry, is its lack of inconsistency with any among the set of definitions, axioms, and postulates, consistently underlying that geometry at each and every possible location within the geometry as a whole. Such a set of definitions, axioms, and postulates, or any substitute for such a set, defines an hypothesis. Each case, in which a new discovery of principle obliges us to change one or more among the set of definitions, axioms, and postulates of a pre-established hypothesis, generates a new hypothesis, which has no deductive consistency with its predecessor. Such orderable successions of hypotheses, imply a parallel to the evolutionary development of mutually distinct, successive species of living creatures. In both cases, the measurable impact of success, is of the form of true "anti-entropy," not the silly definition of "negentropy" employed by Wiener et al. for so-called "information theory."

35. Prince Philip's claim, that the natural father of his children was a great ape, pertains not to the suggestive form of Prince Charles' ears, but to the nature of Prince Philip's co-sponsorship, with ex-Nazi Prince Bernhard of the Netherlands, of both the 1961 founding of the pro-bestial World Wildlife Fund (WWF), and of the revival of Edward VII's "Club of the Isles," as the "1001 Club," the organization created for propagating and funding the spread of the WWF's effort to de-nature the human species. See Mark Burdman, "'Jury' Votes Equal Rights to Apes," *Executive Intelligence Review*, Jan. 26, 1996.

36. The evidence of a perfected design of throwing-spear, dated to an ancient site deep within a mine in Germany, is typical of the evidence pointing to the implied existence of the specifically human genotype, as early as between one and two millions years ago. As in long-range economic forecasting, so in paleontology, it is not sufficient to consider the genetically determined form of hominid-like types; one must seek evidence which could not have been produced except by those kinds of cognitive processes, which set the human species absolutely apart from, and above the higher apes. Compare this with the method identified in Lyndon H. LaRouche, Jr., "Any Enemy of LaRouche Is an Enemy of Clinton," *Executive Intelligence Review*. April 3, 1998. See the section subtitled, "Look to the stars," pp. 28-29. A chimpanzee is able to learn,

of this distinction, is the combination of artifacts which meet the experimental-scientific standard of technologies necessarily born of valid discovery of physical principle, or, which are works conforming to Classical standards for artistic composition.[37] Like the comparison of two observed trajectories of a celestial entity, the congruence of a suspected paleontological specimen of humanity with actual humanity, requires credible agreement in respect of form, but, also, evidence of the relevant, specific, non-linear characteristic of practice. Not accidentally, this is also the principle of competent, long-range economic forecasting.

In respect to physical science, this historical view of the human species' cultural self-development, is marked by a series of known, or necessarily implied particular, validated discoveries of principle. Among the earliest truly interesting expressions of this, are ancient solar-astronomical calendars, containing reasonably accurate long cycles of a thousand years or much more. The pre-Vedic and Vedic such calendars, internally dated to earlier than 4,000 B.C., as addressed by Bal Gangadhar Tilak, are exemplary.[38]

In respect to developed notions of physical science as such, we have the legacy of European Classical-humanist modes of education, such as those practiced by the Brothers of the Common Life, or the Schiller-Humboldt program employed for Nineteenth-Century, and later, German Classical secondary education. That education traced the origins of modern European physical science, from its Classical Greek roots, using a notion of mathematics centered upon the reflections of the work of the school of Pythagoras, of Thales, and of Plato, in the Thirteen Books of Euclid. It employed that same method in search of the relationship between Classical Greek developments, and those of relevant non-Greek predecessors. Out of this approach, modern European civilization developed a rather precise insight, into the notions of which validated discoveries of physical principle must be viewed as successors of some others, and forerunners of still others.[39]

In principle, the potential for a similar sense of ordering of discovery of Classical-artistic principles exists, but is far less developed than is the case for the mathematical-physics domain.[40] Nonetheless, in the

---

and to transmit to offspring, the use of a stick for gathering termites, etc.; the chimpanzee could not discover a physical principle of the type underlying a family of synthesizable technologies. Hence, the design of an ancient throwing spear may serve, as in the cited instance, as dating the existence of a mind of the modern human type.

37. My use of "Classical" always conforms to the standard of Classical Greece, and, most emphatically, to the principle of the *idea* as defined by Plato's method of Socratic dialectic. In respect to art, this always signifies, that the method of characteristic feature of action expressed by the composition of the artistic work, is Classical metaphor, that of the type banned by empiricist Thomas Hobbes, et al. The contrast of Greek Classical art, on this account, to preceding Archaic forms of Egyptian and Greek plastic art-forms, is exemplary.

38. *Orion, or Researches into the Antiquity of the Vedas* (1893), and, its sequel, *The Arctic Home in the Vedas* (1903). Tilak employed studies of Vedic astronomy supplied from German astrophysicists, chiefly from the circles of Carl Gauss. Johannes Kepler was among the first to recognize the astrophysical significance of very long cycles in Vedic solar-astronomical calendars. In contrast to the Vedic-Sanskrit and Egyptian astronomy, that of Mesopotamia is relatively degenerate; like its wicked theology, ancient Mesopotamia leaned more to the lunatic side of precise accounting practices, than the epistemological spirit of scientific inquiry. Curiously tangled, are the facts, that the rudiments of civilization were introduced to the savages of ancient Mesopotamia by the Dravidian colonists from "Harappa" culture, who established Sumer. Thus, the satanic form of religious belief—the cult of Ishtar— specific to Akkadian culture, is, like the kindred religions of ancient Sheba, Ethiopia, and Canaan, and the Hellenistic cult of Isis-Osiris, a reflection of the Shakti-Siva cult, as Herodotus accurately pin-points the Dravidian origins of the pagan religions of Mesopotamia, Sheba, and Canaaan. On this and related accounts, the fusion of the Vedic culture from Central Asia, with the technologically advanced Dravidian, mari-

time culture of Harrapa, etc., contains some riddles of significance for understanding the state of humanity in the Indian Ocean littoral, during the long period, during and immediately following the last great cycle of glaciation. Happily, the conclusions we employ here are not encumbered by such fascinating riddles.

39. One might say, a notion of the *cardinality*, in the sense of the Sieve of Eratosthenes, associated with such ordering of discovered principles.

40. Paradigmatic, is the case of the sequence for Classical music: J.S. Bach, Josef Haydn, Wolfgang Mozart, Josef Haydn after approximately 1786, Beethoven, Schubert, F. Mendelssohn, R. Schumann, and J. Brahms. Once the significance of implicit intervallic inversions was more adequately appreciated, the development of a rigorous polyphony attuned to the natural mode (e.g., Florentine *bel canto*) of the human voice, required the development of polyphonic-voice-determined well-tempered scales set at C=256, rather than the merely equal-tempered values which might be thought to meet the requirements of keyboard instruments. This development of well-tempered polyphony by Bach, already produced the germ of later Classical motivic thorough-composition in Bach's compositions, most notably in such scientific-artistic breakthroughs as Bach's *A Musical Offering*, and the principles of mastery of the role of inversions in well-tempered polyphony, in his *The Art of the Fugue*. Indirectly, as Maestro Norbert Brainin discovered, this led Haydn to the first formal use of this new method of composition in his Opus 33 "Russian" string quartets. Haydn's Opus 33 prompted Mozart to recognize a more advanced version of this approach to motivic thorough-composition, as already realized in essence by J.S. Bach's *A Musical Offering*. Haydn, in turn, then adopted his former student's, Mozart's, discovery in his later works. Beethoven, a student of J.S. Bach's work, adopted Mozart and Haydn, successively, as his chosen teachers. He perfected Mozart's original discovery, establishing this derivative of Bach's work and influence as the foundation for all Classical motivic thorough-composition, through the concluding com-

Classical educational program's artistic curriculum, the principle of education was the same. The student must not *learn* the description of the principle, or the mere use of procedures associated with it; the student must, in his, or her own mind, re-enact the personal, private mental experience of the original discoverer, the strife of resolving ontological paradoxes, that strife which is the form of mental activity from which every valid discovery of principle—in science, or art—is derived.

As in science, so in the domain of great Classical artistic compositions, the student whose talent is developed by Classical-humanist, rather than "drill and grill" modes, *usually* knows the name of the person, whether from the present century, or even several millennia past, who is identified as the original discoverer of reference. That student *always* knows the ontological paradox whose solution is the discovered principle: otherwise, the student could not have experienced the relevant mental act of discovery; otherwise, the student does not *know* the principle, but, at best, has merely tucked it into his "memory banks," has merely *learned* it as mere "information," not knowledge. The graduate of such education also knows which principles of science, or art, or both, he, or she, must have known, prior to undertaking the solution for the relevant paradox. In all such cases, the name for ontological paradox in Classical art-forms, is *metaphor*.

Thus, there are three qualities included in a former student's knowledge of any validated principle of science or art. First, the identity, perhaps even the actual name of the original discoverer of the principle. Second, the paradox, or metaphor, which prompts the regeneration of the principle. Third, the prerequisites for undertaking the attempted solution of that paradox, or metaphor: the notions of *ordering* and *cardinality* common

to both physical science and Classical art.

These considerations, integral outgrowths of the 1948-1951 phase of my work on the project, led to 1952 studies of the work of Georg Cantor,[41] and, then, the rereading of Riemann's 1854 habilitation dissertation[42] as an alternative to Cantor's approach to the notion of the "transfinite."

The problem posed by the outcome of the 1948-1951 interval, was: how to express the progress flowing from scientific and artistic progress, in functional terms which might be correlated with relevant measurements. The fact, that both scientific and Classical-artistic principles, represented an implicitly orderable sequence of expanding, multiply-connected manifolds, was key to the solution. Riemann's recasting of both Leibniz's and Gauss's preceding work, on the overcoming of the fallacies inhering in an aprioristic form of geometry, provided the key for solving the problem. Most notable was Riemann's explicit freeing of physics from the shackles of formalist mathematics: the notion of the unique, experimentally determined relationship between an n-fold physical manifold, and some measurable characteristic of action within the physical domain actually corresponding to such a manifold. In other words, with each discovery of principle, we must create a new mathematics, to replace the old, and must determine the characteristic of action within that new manifold experimentally, as Wilhelm Weber, for example, did for microphysics, in the instance of his experimental proof-of-principle for Ampère's "longitudinal force."[43]

In this connection, I added two new features to the Riemannian form of representation of a physical-economic hyper-manifold, determined by scientific and technological progress. The less revolutionary of these two additions, was the use of my own definition of physical-economic anti-entropy, in terms of a form of systems of simultaneous inequalities, whose result may be represented in linear terms, but which is not linked functionally to any linear system.[44] The second, which is, formally, far more radical, of course, was to superimpose an m-fold manifold, of discoveries of Classical-artistic principles, including principles of history in the

---

position by Johannes Brahms, and beyond. None would have been possible, without the work of his relevant predecessors. The same applies to Classical tragedy, in the succession: Aeschylus, Shakespeare, and Schiller, each of whom rested explicitly on the work of the relevant predecessors. In poetry, without the Classical Greek models, as opposed to the predominantly more trivial Latin models, Classical European poetry would not have come into existence. In plastic art-forms, without the revolution exemplified by the transmissions of the revolutionary principle, away from the Archaic, provided by the work of Scopas and Praxiteles, a Leonardo da Vinci, Raphael, or Rembrandt, would not have been conceivable. Rather than "four-square" tombstone designs, or pathetically symbolic "primitives" with no coherent principle, the Classical plastic art-forms express a degree of metaphorical imbalance, which forces the mind to adduce motion—change—rather than a naive, static imagery.

41. Georg Cantor, *Beiträge zur Begründung der transfiniten Mengenlehre,* in Ernst Zermelo, ed., ***Georg Cantors gesammelte Abhandlungen*** (Hildesheim: Georg Olms Verlag, 1962).

42. See footnote 33.

43. Ibid.

44. ***So, You Wish to Learn All About Economics?*** op. cit.

large, upon any given n-fold manifold of validated physical principles. Thus, I redefined experimental science, as the experimental testing of the validity of principles of Classical art and history, in terms of the human species' required, anti-entropic form of increase of its per-capita, per-square-kilometer power over the universe.

With the combining of those two elements, in that fashion, I shifted the question from the experimental testing of a presented candidate to become a scientific principle, to a testing of the validity of those cognitive habits, by means of which both successful discoveries of principle, and the experimental validation of those discoveries, are generated by the individual human mind. In other words, the primary subject-matter became that which can be known, but can not be represented in terms of sense-perception.

This brings Classical education back into focus, once again.

In the process of Classical education, the student re-experiences original discoveries of physical principle, Classical art-forms, and history itself, as if the student had been the relevant original discoverer. The scope of this education reaches, implicitly, toward the contributions to knowledge of principle gained by all previous human existence. Although the number of principles known in this way, may be limited, they are representative of the net outcome of the history of knowledge to the present time. The student becomes, thus, in that degree, a living embodiment of all prior human existence: *an actual world-historical individual.*

That has a directly relevant connotation for the matter immediately at hand. In the given case, the student is doing something far more profound, than merely coming to *know* (rather than merely having learned) a collection of validated principles. The student has repeated the act of successful cognitive solution for paradoxes (e.g., metaphors). In this way, the student has relived the relevant movements, from within the mind of the relevant original discoverer. The graduate of such an education must be cautious in his, or her selection of a future mate, lest he or she come to find, that one knows the most intimate facets of moments from the minds of many original discoverers, far better than one knows who is really behind the face of one's marriage-partner. The relevant student has repeated many times the greatest experiment of all, to prove the validity, the reliability of that agency which is the cognitive creative powers of the individual

human mind, the powers better understood, only when one has perfected them considerably through many, many honings of their cutting edge.

This role of Classically-educated cognition, comes into focus in science and society, once we attempt to locate the "in-betweenness," which connects two, successively developed, formally inconsistent manifolds. How does something higher, develop out of something lesser? How does something totally irreconcilable, deductively, with its starting-point, develop out of that starting-point? Obviously, no manifold produces such successors. The transformation occurs from outside that original manifold, a transformation which is caused by, and which conforms to those creative cognitive processes which correspond to no sense-perceptual representation. It is the development of those innate potentials for successful creative cognition, which is the only valid purpose of a good education. The student so benefitted, comes to the state of familiarity with, and experimentally grounded confidence in those specific, sovereign cognitive powers of the developed individual mind, in which he, or she is able to call those powers into play, once again, at will.[45]

Restate this crucial point. What is the ordering-principle, which governs the successful generation of a validated new manifold, out of the prompting of this discovery, by the ontological paradoxes of the superseded manifold? What is the agency which performs this action? It is the developed cognitive powers of the individual human mind, cognitive powers which absolutely defy simply sense-perceptual, or algebraic forms of representation. *This transformation is the source of anti-entropy, contributed to the physical-economic and related social processes by individual cognitive creativity.*

There is a further implication in that. The peculiarity of man's relationship to the universe at large, is expressed most succinctly, by the fact that whenever the human cognitive processes generate a validatable discovery of principle, the universe is so designed that it is self-obliged to submit more fully to mankind's will on

---

45. A couple decades past, Dr. Stephen Pepper chanced to meet the Dr. Lawrence S. Kubie on whose work I had bestowed much praise: qualified praise, but, despite his association with Freudian psychoanalysis, well-deserved praise. In the course of the brief exchange between Pepper and Kubie, Kubie insisted, quite rightly, that creativity is a good in and of itself. If we may read that observation as consistent with what I have just stated here, the late Dr. Kubie was certainly correct in that opinion.

that specific account. It is this anti-entropic quality characteristic of the individual cognitive processes, which is the source of the power compelling such obedience from nature. *Such is the nature of the fundamental ordering principles of the universe.*

The Morality of Classical Education

Until the Jacobin atrocities launched in France, beginning July 14, 1789, the most moral citizens of Europe were inspired by the example of the U.S. Declaration of Independence, the ensuing struggle for liberty against the evil tyranny of the British monarchy, and the U.S. Federal Constitution. To any literate German—the members of the pro-U.S.A. *Lesergesellschaften*, for example—the Declaration of Independence and Preamble of the Federal Constitution, were reflections of the anti-Locke philosophy of Gottfried Leibniz. At the outbreak of the French Revolution, these republican strata of Europe hoped that the result would be the rapid spread of the U.S. example into Europe. With the increasingly menacing atrocities led by such Anglophile revolutionaries as Maximilien Robespierre and the Duke of Orléans, Philippe Egalité, and then, the escalation of the Terror under outright British agents Danton and Marat, a terrible depression settled upon Europe over the years 1789-1794, preceding the July 1794 toppling of the terrorist regime of Robespierre and Saint-Just.

To translate somewhat freely Friedrich Schiller's famous remark on these developments in France: "A great moment has found a little people." The want of a moral development in the French population, had turned opportunity into catastrophe. On this account, Schiller led in pointing to the importance of a Classical education of the population, education based upon not only science, but also the role of great examples of Classical art-forms, in effecting the moral education of the mental faculties. Unfortunately, especially since the cultural downshift of 1964-1972, the which has been accompanied by a virtual extinction of popular participation in Classical art-forms, a state of widespread moral illiteracy, has become "mainstream thinking" in both Europe and the Americas. Once again, a great moment of crisis, a great opportunity for long-needed change, finds among the leaders and population of these nations, a "little people," akin to the perilous moral condition of the 1789-1794 population of France.

Under such conditions, only the most exceptional type of leadership, can successfully guide a self-imperilled nation, or nations, to an historical place of safety. In such a circumstance, such qualities of leadership are distinguished for the egregiousness with which their proposed, indispensable remedies, are regarded, and resisted by both leading institutions, and much of the population in general.

These kinds of problems were already evident in the U.S. population and institutions during the pre-World War II decades. The influence of pragmatism upon public and higher education, was part of the morally corrosive influence, responsible for undermining the popular moral faculties. More broadly, there was the spread of populism, which placed ignorant, and usually false, commonplace opinions and tastes, above relevant cultivated knowledge. The most widespread fear was the fear of becoming "unpopular," of expressing "unpopular opinions," exhibiting "unpopular" tastes. The adolescent girl or boy, usually prized becoming "the most popular" of their gender, and usually feared— sometimes to the extreme degree of social-theorist Emile Durkheim's notion of *anomie*—a lack of such status. The desire of most such young folk, of my own and the succeeding generation, to be something worthwhile, was superseded by a pitiable, romantic fascination with looking like, or smelling like, some movie-idol. The essential moral quality, the strength to stand alone for truth and justice, against wrongful popular opinion, was undermined, and, after developments of 1964-1972, virtually, lost somewhere in a vast stinking swamp of "political correctness."

These matters belong to what I have identified here, as earlier, as the m-fold set of artistic postulates, which shape the way in which the mind guides both the cognitive act of validatable discovery, and the way in which social relations react to such discoveries. Look at the internal dynamics of Classical artistry from this point of reference. After a relatively brief treatment of that sub-aspect of our topic here, we shall return, prepared, to examine the nature of the interactions between the m-fold and n-fold manifolds.

Take the case of performance of Classical musical compositions. Look at the moral root-difference between a Classical performance of Bach, Mozart, Beethoven, Schubert, Chopin, Schumann, or Brahms, and an attempt to read such a composition in the Romantic mode, as if it had been composed by Franz Liszt or Richard Wagner. The essence of the difference in approach, is between an *agapic* passion, like that associated with the joy of effecting a valid scientific, or related discovery of truth, or realization of justice denied—as against the alternative, *erotic* passion of mere sensual effects.

To this end, consider the case of the Classical composition: The performer's or performers' attack upon the opening tone and first interval of the composition is decisive. The beginning of the composition defines a musical statement, which serves as the take-off point for the process of development of the composition in its polyphonic entirety. The performer must not only seize the audience's attention at the outset, but must grip that attention in a way consistent with the process of development which, in the end, becomes the idea of the composition as a unified, indivisible entirety. The late Wilhelm Furtwängler was a master of this.

This problem confronts the Classical performer in one way, and the Romantic in another; despite the differences, the attack upon the opening, is more or less decisive for the audience's apprehended artistic impact of the composition as whole. In the first instance, the Classical evocation of *agapē*,[46] is associated with the characteristic feature of great Classical compositions, since the relevant work of J.S. Bach: motivic, polyphonic thorough-composition. This reflects, thus, the quality of anti-entropy. In contrast, the anarchic sensualism of Romantic, Modern, and post-Modern art, appeals only to a linear emotion, that of lust and rage.

At first reading of my argument here so far, it might be suggested that art is only another expression of the same quality of discovery, met in validated discoveries of physical principle. That would be a superficial interpretation of the actual connections between science and Classical art. By physical science, we mean the relationship between the individual cognitive processes, and the individual's ability to act efficiently upon the physical universe. In art, we employ the same cognitive faculties, to the same included effect, but with crucial social dimensions added.

From the standpoint of validated original discoveries of physical principle, the first social problem encountered by a valid discovery, is the challenge of replicating that cognitive act in the mind of another person,

i.e. Classical modes of education. The leading consideration is, that the cognitive processes of cognitive discovery by one person, can not be perceived, nor represented within the bounds of sense-perception. The only way those cognitive processes can be defined as a mental object of knowledge, is to replicate the validated process of discovery by another, in one's own cognitive processes. It is this deeper aspect of human social relations, rather than the form of relations located within the more superficial domain of sense-perception, which is the essential character of social relations overall.

Thus, in art, we apply the quality of cognitive passion associated with validatable discoveries of physical principle, to social relations as such. The general theme of this interplay, is the conflict between the agapic passion of creative cognitive processes, and erotic impulses associated with mere sensuality, with sense-perception as such. The characteristic problem, so posed, is the struggle to maintain the agapic mood's efficient subordination of erotic impulses to agapic purposes.[47]

In Classical art-forms, this social relationship is expressed always as a metaphor. This is the "To be [*agapē*], or not to be [*eros*]," of the Third Act soliloquy by Shakespeare's Hamlet. Or, in Schiller's counsel, the audience departing the theater after the performance of a Classical tragedy, must leave the theater better people than they had entered it. These desiderata are the key to all great Classical artistic compositions. It is the reading of history from this Classical-artistic vantage-point, which is the truth of history. It is the same, differently located, in Classical musical composition, as best exemplified by the greatest Classical polyphony.

Thus, so informed by Classical art, we approach the practical matters of life with our passions made literate. The motive so supplied, is to realize truth and justice in society. The notion of truth and justice is located in an (agapically) impassioned prescience of the necessity for that anti-entropic progress of mankind, which is the characteristic of the agapic, otherwise known as creative-cognitive mood.

Art and Hypothesis

The scientific approach to physical economy, is motivated by concern to foster forms of progress which improve the potential relative population-density of mankind. This improvement depends upon what we

---

46. *Agapē* as defined by Plato, the passion which compels one to accept nothing less than truth and justice, is the same quality of *agapē* referenced by the Apostle Paul's *I Corinthians* 13. It is, therefore, the passion for truth, which supplies the needed energy for the quality of concentration required to transform an ontological paradox, or Classical metaphor, into a validatable discovery of principle.

47. If you will, you make take this as a reading of Paul's *I Corinthians* 13.

call investment in scientific and technological progress, which means, in the relatively longer term, revolutionary transformations from an initial science-manifold of n principles, to successive new manifolds, of, successively, n+1, n+2,..., principles. There are two leading problems posed by this consideration.

The first of these two problems, is the science-driver principle itself. Each transition, from an n-fold, to an n+1-fold manifold, requires cognitive action. In other words, the specifically anti-entropic intervention, by cognition, which is the unique origin of upward ordering of successive, anti-entropic transformations of scientific hypothesis. Without a high degree of agapic development among scientists and related strata, this ordering will not appear as desired.

The second of these two problems, is the society's attitude toward such scientific and technological progress. The questions include: How is this to be fostered? How are the benefits to be applied? What is the moral purpose toward which this effort is directed? What is the nature of the individual member of the human species, such that we are obliged to steer society's development and related practice in one certain direction, rather than another? In short, the set of implicit moral values distributed among members and strata of the population, will act, and with passion, to shape the direction of policy-decisions, according to the social values placed on alternative proposed answers to those questions.

In the case of the outstanding progress of western European civilization, from the Fifteenth-Century Golden Renaissance into much of the troubled Twentieth Century, the driving passion was that specific to western European Christianity: the emphasis upon struggling against the legacies of Babylon and of the evil Roman and Byzantine empires, and also against feudalism, to establish a form of society cohering with the notion that all persons, without racial or ethnic distinction permitted, are equally made in the image of God, that evidenced by the creative powers of cognition, awaiting development in each new-born personality.

The notion of society's obligation to develop those powers, and to rely upon them as the source of solutions for great problems, is the driving passion which engendered that European form of modern sovereign nation-state republic, best expressed by the Declaration of Independence and Preamble of the Federal Constitution of the young United States, a U.S. whose peculiar advantages were, that it was an embodiment of the best ideas produced in Europe, such as those of Leibniz, in particular, but ideas expressed at a strategically less insecure position, relative to the long arms of those feudal relics known as the European landed aristocracy and financier oligarchy.

Thus, to forecast, one must concentrate on both the physical-economic aspect, with its immediate connections to matters of principles of physical science, but also the generationally oriented social-cultural processes. We have a significant, but secondary interest in the relatively more transient opinions as such, but a great deal of interest in what the London Tavistock Institute would prefer to identify as cultural "mind-set," or "cultural paradigm shifts:" the axiomatic hypotheses which tend to predetermine what opinions will be engendered, by the unfolding of a certain direction in combined, interacting, cultural and physical-economic developments over, usually, the span of a generation or two.

One can not master forecasting of this sort from an "ivory tower." In the absence of the existence of determinable, precise magnitudes of passion, associated with the set of any cultural paradigm, forecasting demands a high degree of intellectual participation in the process of studying patterns of shifts within populations, a study which must be grounded, inclusively, in an intense study of history from this vantage-point.

As a forecaster, my advantages have included, prominently, my critical view of the cultural quality of various strata among the populations of, most notably, North America and western Europe. This engagement, grounded in Classical philosophy, made it possible to foresee how institutions and populations would react to the very developments their own cultural impulses would prompt. A strong trend in culture will usually drive to some limit, at which it imposes a crisis upon itself; how it will respond to the crisis its choice of cultural impulse itself has thus caused, has been the usual record of history.

The first thing in successful long-range forecasting, is to recognize that the problem of forecasting as I have outlined it here, exists. Thus, to put aside the simplistic, usually reductionist, fallacy of composition, which has usually passed for economic forecasting methods in modern professional education and government.